Praise for Kicking the BIG BUT Syndrome®

"Kicking the Big BUT is the Big Breakthrough we have been waiting for. This book contains everything you need to live the life of your dreams. By following the guidance provided by Soul Intuitive Eddie Conner, you can have everything in life you ever wanted; from a loving relationship with your mate to improving your relationship with money and career, and your creator."

—Victor Benoun
—Author of *Your Castle, No Hassle*

"Author Eddie Conner empowers his readers to get off their ass and kick The BIG BUT Syndrome by leaving their <u>BUTs</u> behind and making their dreams come true with simple tools and loving humor."

—Jacquie Jordon
—TV Producer/Media Consultant

"After reading Eddie's unique and funny perspective on how we all can self-sabotage ourselves with our BIG BUTS, I am ready to look my BIG BUT in the mirror and make some changes. With humorous stories, insightful observations and great depth, Eddie coaches and cheer-leads us all to a place

*where we have choices and freedom to be, do, and have what
we want in life—NO BUTS about it!"*

—Karen Drucker
—Inspirational Recording Artist

*"Eddie Conner can kick my BIG BUT anytime! Being a
writer myself, I truly appreciate the simplicity of using BUT
armor "Punctuation Shields" like the period to stop a contradicted desire in its path—it's so simple. Now try using
"and" to link your first desire with another pure, joyful,
focused intention! Eddie's techniques empower you to feel
good, appreciate all you have, and kick BUT big time.
Thank you for your light and energy."*

—Arlene Zimmerly
—Author of *Gregg College Keyboarding & Document
Processing and Keyboarding Connections*

*"Eddie, Thank You for helping us all realize that life doesn't
have to be about our BIG BUTS!"*

—Taaffe C. O'Connell
—Actress/Publisher/Named Who's Who in the World

*"Don't let the humor, warmth, and down-home flavor of
Eddie Conner's Big But Syndrome fool you; he shares some
seriously important, and liberating wisdom. Never before*

has so much light been wonderfully shined on one of the biggest thought-nullifiers in our vocabulary. Well done!"

—Adam Abraham

—Publisher/Author of *I Am My Body, NOT!*

"Eddie Conner teaches us to hold up the "OVAL Mirror" of life so we can see our "Big Buts". Through humor and clever techniques we learn to kick our "Big But Syndrome". With Eddie's book of knowledge for life, there is no excuse for us not to have the heavenly life we have always dreamed of!"

—Mary Ann Halpin

—Acclaimed Photographer/Author of

Pregnant Goddesshood

"By following Eddie's advice in this lively, funny book, I was able to kick my own BUT problem and begin living a richer, fuller, BUT—free life!"

—Brian A. Wilson

—Hollywood Writer/Director

"This book shows you how to get your beliefs and your desires on the same energy level. From this new perspective, you will be able to soar your way to success."

—John Livesay

—Author of *The 7 Most Powerful Selling Secrets*

"Eddie Conner has written an exuberant, enlightening book on the "Yeah buts" that muddle up our thinking and stop us from our good. When your BIG BUT gets you down, pick up this entertaining treasure filled with wonderful tools to lighten your load."

—Chellie Campbell
—Author of *The Wealthy Spirit*

Kicking the BIG BUT
Syndrome®

Kicking the BIG BUT Syndrome®

Eddie Conner

iUniverse, Inc.
New York Lincoln Shanghai

Kicking the BIG BUT Syndrome®

iUniverse, Inc.

For information address:
iUniverse, Inc.
2021 Pine Lake Road, Suite 100
Lincoln, NE 68512
www.iuniverse.com

ISBN: 0-595-32181-X

Printed in the United States of America

I dedicate this book to my Mom and soul mate
Ann Crews,
You have always been my first and
greatest source of inspiration.
I love you.

Contents

Section Two: The **SOUL***ution*

Acknowledgements

I want to thank my amazing friend Victor Benoun for encouraging me to transform a two-page class outline into this book. I am grateful to my dream team: Mike and Ramona Mucciolo, Rose Wuyts-Wilson, Brian A. Wilson, Jeff Dannels, Cynthia Cavalcanti, Cynthia Richmond, Barbara Adams, and Robert Villegas for your endless hours of love, creativity, and professional guidance.

Special thanks still to Chellie Campbell, John Livesay, Karen Drucker, Taaffe C. O'Connell, Jacquie Jordon, Arlene Zimmerly, Mary Ann Halpin, Rev. Maureen Hoyt, Adam Abraham, James Cass Rogers, Shakti Gawain, Carolina Mariposa, Lauren Soloman, Krista Allen, Arlene Morse, Mary B. Aversano, Evelyn Villegas, Tim Mann, Debbie Mangum, Ellen Dostal, David Tillman, Kathy Gordon, Allison Cash, DJ Mitch, David Ault, Karen Newton, Cherry Lea, Karen Moriuchi, Janice Acquaviva, Melissa McFarland, Jill Lloyd, Marissa Kelley, Jeff Mayse, Nick Florez, RJ Durell, Tammi, Shawn Kindorf, Becky Moore, Innerchange Magazine, Dancing Moon Books & Gifts, Phoenix Rising Bookstore and to all my friends, clients, and associates! I could not have accomplished a project of this magnitude without your continued love and support. No Buts About It!

◆   ◆   ◆

I want to send a special note of appreciation to my most influential spiritual teacher, Abraham-Hicks, for being pure, passionate teachers. Your wisdom is loving, healing, and life-changing. I attribute my ability to complete this project directly to your priceless message that we all have the power to change our physical circumstances with our invisible attributes. Thank you for the light you generously share with millions.

Foreword

It is so fitting that this book is written by Eddie Conner. I have known Eddie for a decade, and he never disappoints me in his ability to choose to feel good and make all those around him feel good too. Eddie is a magnet for powerfully positive thoughts and feelings. You just cannot be around him and not be laughing and playing and having a great time. But Eddie is serious about feeling good. There is a science behind his claims, and there are powerful "manifestors", like myself, who have used Eddie's techniques and attracted exactly what they wanted for their lives.

Someone so happy must have been born into the perfect circumstances, right? Not Eddie. In fact, he was born in a less-than-ideal situation and he was truly grateful for every blessing that came his way. Through his innate intuition, humor, and desire to make his mama happy, Eddie learned to recognize the positive side of everything. Science would later support his idea that we are living in a hologram that is a reflection of our expectations and intentions. The more sweet, positive, and loving thoughts and feelings we send out, the more we receive.

If your world is a hostile, unforgiving, and apathetic place, ask yourself, "Where am I feeling hostile?" and send forth compassion; "Who do I need to forgive?" and let the slight go; and, "What don't I care about?" and learn something about that thing. When you bring joy to others, you will feel joy. You cannot avoid it. Conversely, when you contradict your dreams and goals with a BIG BUT, you cancel any way the Creator of the Creation has of delivering up your order.

Eddie makes this lesson a fabulously fun course of study. Remember when Mary Poppins sang, "A spoonful of sugar makes the medicine go down"? *Kicking the BIG BUT Syndrome* is a sweet way of helping us accept a bitter truth, i.e., that we sabotage ourselves. And through wisdom, exercises, and suggestions, it provides the remedy. You can heal this syndrome, and the medicine is in this book. You are holding the miracle cure for your life. Get ready to laugh and love and grow rich.

Cynthia Richmond

Author of *Dream Power: Use Your Night Dreams to Change Your Life*

Preface

When I called Mom and told her I was working on a book, she was thrilled. Then I told her the material was called, "The Big BUT Syndrome."

There was a deafening silence on the other end of the phone.

"Mom?" I said.

Chirping crickets seemed to fill the 2,600 miles between my place in Los Angeles and my mother's home in High Point, North Carolina.

"Mom, it's a cool idea. It'll help a lot of people."

There are times when you don't really want peace and quiet. This was one of those times! At last, Mom cleared her throat. "Edward," she began, pausing for dramatic effect as mothers often do.

My imagination took off as if someone had fired a starter's pistol. My mind raced, across the country and back through time, until I was a child again, growing up in "the Projects" of North Carolina. Looking back, it seems like a tough place to start. But at the time, it was all I knew, and Mom made it home for me and my brothers.

When I was five, we "moved on up" to a mobile home. A single-wide, if you must know! Yep, no kidding—I lived in a trailer park. Again, not the nicest living conditions perhaps, but it gave me the greatest of luxuries: time. I had a lot of time to sit and think and just...be. It was during this time that I started to realize I heard things, saw things that my wacky brothers and overbearing father did not see. My psychic abilities were making themselves known to me.

Daydreaming and tapping into my psychic impressions helped me escape the crushing poverty and violence of my childhood.

As I moved into high school, I started to realize my gifts could help others answer questions and solve problems related to their own lives. That made them feel good, and I realized it made me feel good and gave me purpose.

I had a string of "regular" jobs—fry cook at Sizzler, calendar machine operator (please, don't ask!) in the textile mill—but none of them gave me the satisfaction I was after. It was time to seek out something more.

With some urging from my best friend, Tim, I packed my bags, said my good-byes, kissed my Mom and moved to Los Angeles.

I came to Dreamland to pursue my dreams. During my eight years here in the city of angels, I've tapped deeper into my psychic abilities, enhanced my "soul awareness" and have helped hundreds of people reshape their lives. Living my dreams was helping other people live theirs!

The more people I helped, the more I noticed a pattern in their lives. The biggest problem people have isn't any lack of ability or lack of desire or any other lack; it seems to me their biggest problem is getting in their own way. And what gets in our way the most? Our big BUTS: the BUTS that stop us, the BUTS that slow us down, the BUTS that make us hesitate.

I want to get rid of every "BUT" in America! And this book is my way of doing exactly that, one BUT at a time...starting with *your* "BUT"!

Everything I've come to understand, every good and bad and humbling and exhilarating experience I've had since I was an eight-year-old boy in North Carolina, sitting on a rusty oil drum and watching fall leaves drift by, is incorporated into this book.

Mom's voice stopped my racing mind and brought me back into the moment. "Edward," she continued, "What if the Big But Syndrome becomes a national phenomenon? Are you sure you want to be known across the country as the guy who spends his life worrying about Big Buts?"

I said that nothing would make me happier.

"Well then, go on and do it, Edward," Mom said. "I'll be very proud of you."

And she didn't say "but" once. Now that is a mother's love.

What you hold in your hands is my life and its lessons. I hope they help you lead a richer, fuller, happier life. I hope this book enlightens you, and relieves you of your own Big But.

Wishing you peace, prosperity, and a BUT-free existence,
Eddie Conner
Los Angeles, California

P.S. Throughout the book, you'll notice several illustrations of a donkey wearing a sandwich board. That's Ralph the BUT donkey. Actually, he's not a donkey, he's an ass, which is what our BUTS can turn us into if we don't watch out. So be nice to Ralph the Ass, and remember: while Ralph may be stuck being an ass, you can always get rid of your BUT!

A Note to the Reader

This book is divided into two segments, The Problem and the Solution. First of all, we will present and identify the Problem Section, which discusses the epidemic of the BIG BUT Syndrome and how we are anal about the usage of our BIG BUTS. The second section joyously offers creative Solutions to our much-deserved desires, while also sharing Soul Tools that will enhance your practical daily living.

It is my desire that one day soon, as you experience a mild problem, you will choose to utilize your human-soul potential first and put your old habits of thinking on the back burner. This alone will change your life in miraculous ways.

Enjoy.

Introduction

○ ○

To believe is to be strong. Doubt cramps energy. Belief is power.

—Frederick William Robertson

Humans are the only species on this planet that contradicts desires with a variety of negative belief patterns. As a result, we are the only physical entities who can and do get ourselves caught in the trappings of the BIG BUT Syndrome®.

According to the U.S. Census Bureau, the population in our country was 281,421,906 in the year 2000. Now, that's a lot of people in one location. It's no wonder the acreage we lived on as children has greatly reduced in size and tripled in value in such a short span of time.

Every minute, at least one million Americans are infected with the BIG BUT Syndrome®, and every hour, the dreams of another five million people are either contaminated or terminated in this epidemic of contradicted beliefs.

Are you one of the millions of people working long hours to make your dreams a reality, BUT you can't seem to get where you want to go? Have you ever felt there was an invisible force holding you back from your long-awaited goals and aspirations? If so, you know what it feels like to be trapped in a contradicted vortex of hard work and frustration in which you realize you are not where you deserve to be in life.

Without realizing it, most adults think and talk in a contradictory way about the subjects that are most important to them. They express what they do and do not want in the same sentence or action. A common example of this behavior is when we hear people say things like, "I want a relationship, *but* most men are jerks." If I had a dime for every time I heard that sentence, I could buy a condo with a penthouse view between Bill Gates and Donald Trump.

Another area of contrary desire is money. It is fascinating to observe people talking about lack of, absence of, and not-enough-of money in their lives. The desire for money is abundant enough, BUT the opposing belief to that desire is a poverty consciousness. In many ways, the same conflicted dynamic holds true with our personal beliefs around our careers.

When people seek advice from psychics, coaches, or therapists, they ask about the "Big Three" topics: Love, Money, and Career. These are the most talked about adult topics we engage in with the greatest desire and opposing negative emotion.

Mental note: the next time you are with friends or co-workers, listen and *feel* the frequency or energetic tone of the conversation. You will recognize the difference between hi-frequency and low-frequency dialogue immediately.

A hi-frequency tone ranges from a feel good, to a feel great, to an orgasmic sensation, while a low-frequency interaction ranges from complacency, to mild irritation, to a depressed energy tone.

As we talk about hi-frequency subjects, we attract more hi-frequency people, places, and situations. The same is true with low-frequency dialogues; as we discuss subjects that irritate us, we attract irritating people, places, and situations to us.

While chewing the fat with our buddies, we have a tendency to talk about, think about, and observe the things we do NOT want in life. We think we're talking about what we do want, because we're talking about subject matter that is important to us. However, more often than not, we're verbalizing and vibrating low-grade frequencies. For instance, during work how many times have we congregated at the water cooler to complain with our fellow associates about the neglect of upper management, pay cuts, mistreatment, or the fear of being laid off or worse, fired? In these moments, we are usually radiating a low frequency and observing more of what we do NOT want while we are talking about our job.

The frequency we emanate while communicating our thoughts or our spoken word is always a dead giveaway as to how we truly feel about the subject matter. If we are honestly talking about what we want, we should be feeling good about it—not bad.

Let's stick with relationships. Pretend you are single and out with good friends. The conversation turns to your desire to have a serious intimate relationship, someone to spend the rest of your life with. What is the first thing you and your friends talk about where love and finding the perfect someone to settle down with is concerned?

Did you notice how quickly and easily the conversation eroded into the old "learned" behavior that felt more low-frequency than hi-frequency? Just for fun, have you been in a conversation that sounded something like: "I want a relationship but, I don't want to waste any more time if he/she isn't the right one for me," or "The clock's ticking honey, I can't wait much longer, my eggs are drying up. Yikes, there goes another one! Quick, get me to the freezer!"?

Most adults spend more time imagining, pretending, daydreaming, fantasizing, and believing the impossibilities about our heartfelt, hi-frequency desires. We actively cancel out those positive needs and replace our pure desire with habitual problem-solving and troubleshooting patterns that we use to protect ourselves from repeating the same mistakes from our personal history. Or so we thought!

Where did we learn to contradict our desires?

We inherited this unseen habit of thought from authority figures while growing up. The fruit never falls far from the tree. For the most part, we are the byproducts of our ancestors, and we will more than likely follow in their footsteps. We must make a conscious decision to change our ancestral low-frequency patterns of contradiction to present-moment hi-frequency patterns of pure desire.

When we learn to love without contradicting love with worry, and when we consciously choose to appreciate the money in our pockets right now without complaining that it's not enough, our lives will change in miraculous ways.

The moment we lose our BIG BUTs, we automatically emanate a series of pure, refined energy signals from within us to the heart and soul of the Universe. In return, the Universe can finally bring us what we do want instead of more of what we do not want.

I know all of us are here to create our personal greatness and to joyously carry that greatness in our heart, body language, and spirit.

Tapping into this wellspring of heavenly bliss is easier to accomplish than we realize. It is my intention to offer you many **Soul Instruments** you can easily implement in order to create your desired outcome with love, money, career, and other areas that are important to you.

Section One:
The Problem

1

Defining the BIG BUT Syndrome

Big: Of considerable size, magnitude, large.
But: Contrary to expectation. But introduces a statement in opposition to what precedes it.
Syndrome: any complex of symptoms of the existence of an undesirable condition or quality.

—*American Heritage Dictionary*

The BIG BUT Syndrome®
Having considerable desire with a contradicted belief to that desire, which, over time, creates an unpleasant quality of life.

—*Eddie Conner*

Eleanor Roosevelt said, *"The future belongs to those who believe in the beauty of their dreams."*

As we have already established, the *BIG BUT Syndrome®* is having a considerable desire with a contradicted belief to that desire, which, over time, creates an unpleasant quality of life.

In order to get a strong grasp on the essence of the BIG BUT Syndrome® and how it negatively affects millions of us every second, it is important to amplify its emotional and intellectual aspects. On an intellectual level, the *American Heritage Dictionary* defines Desire and Belief as follows:

9

Desire: To express a wish for. To long for; want; crave.

Belief: Mental acceptance or conviction in the truth or actuality of something. Something believed or accepted as true.

On an intellectual and emotional level, each of us possesses both a desire (Emotion—more of a right-brain attribute) and a belief (Intellect—a left-brain attribute) about every subject known to humankind. Some subjects carry less desire and less belief than others.

First, there is desire (a hi-frequency emotion). We have a desire for unconditional love and for self-love. We have a desire for continued happiness and a desire for financial and spiritual prosperity in our lives and in the lives of those we love. We have a desire to be appreciated and respected and to be treated in an appropriate manner. We have a desire for good health, well-being, and wholeness, to name a few.

For each desire we hold, we also have a belief about that desire! Said belief is either in harmony with or opposed to our desire. If our belief and desire are in harmony, life feels great. And, if we have a desire with an opposing belief, our conscious left brain and subconscious right brain are, in essence, arguing with one another.

Next, there is belief (a perceived fact or truth). We have a belief the sun will continue shining its warm rays upon us. We have a belief there will always be plenty of oxygen to breathe. We have a belief that hummingbirds are magical and otherworldly. Each listed belief is in harmony with the beliefs of the mass majority regarding the subject of hummingbirds, oxygen, and the sun's warm rays.

When we define *desire* and *belief*, giving examples of each, the definitions look and feel simple, *BUT* (pun intended) when we examine desire and belief together in a single subject that is extraordinarily important to us, like love, we frequently experience an emotional struggle rumbling in our gut, or what I like to call the **Solar Plexus Megaphone**®.

For an illustration of hi-frequency desire with an opposing belief, let's recap our previous paragraph on desire. As you read each statement listed below, feel free to write down or to say aloud your personal Belief about each desire.

"I have a *desire* for unconditional love and self-love."

"I have a *desire* for continued happiness and a *desire* for financial and spiritual prosperity in my life and in the lives of those I love."

"I have a *desire* to be appreciated and respected and to be treated in an appropriate manner in all areas of my life."

"I have a *desire* for good health well-being, and wholeness."

Now, I would like to ask you how you are feeling about these statements of desire.

Is your desire for love/self-love in harmony with your existing belief that you can have it? Or do you have a negative belief that is opposing your desire for love? Do you possess hi-frequency desire for love/self-love with a low-frequency belief that you cannot have your desires fulfilled?

What is it about those important areas in life—where both our desire and beliefs are strong and often conflicting—that are causing our desire and our beliefs to put on their psychic boxing gloves and duke it out until the stronger of the two wins the fight? In many cases, the contradicted or opposing belief is usually the winner, thus leaving you and your desire losers in the game of love again.

At last, our big ole BUT enters the scenario. The reason the word BUT is one of my favorite words is its ability to virtually go unnoticed. It is practically invisible, not to mention it is one of the smallest and seemingly non-threatening words in the English language. Each time we use the word BUT, it is likened to the small stone in David's slingshot in the story of David and Goliath. That simple stone represents the power of our BIG BUT. Each time we put a single BUT in the slingshot of our opposing beliefs, it continues to bring down the giant empire of desire living inside us. BUT is almost always the crème sandwiched between the cookie of our desire and the cookie of our belief.

You could be experiencing a monumental avalanche of hi-frequency desire with an equal cataclysm of low-frequency belief in the same thought, sentence, or action. Quietly suspended between these two earth-shattering events is our itsy bitsy, teeny weenie, microscopic BUT, holding steadfast between our desire and our belief. BUT is contrary to expectation, and each BUT introduces a statement in opposition to whatever precedes it.

Let's apply our new knowledge. Since the subject of unconditional love for self and others is a conflicting and confusing area in life, most of my clients ask for clear examples of the BIG BUT Syndrome® in this category.

Patti is a gorgeous thirty-something woman who raised her hand at a *"Create Your Soul Mate"* class I facilitate in the Los Angeles area. The few times she shared in class, it was obvious she was smart, articulate, and had a great sense of humor. With a smile in her voice, she simply stated, "I do want to fall madly in love again *BUT,* I'm afraid of getting hurt." The moment she finished speaking, a few others in our class gave her a series of high fives overlapped with a hearty round of "You Go Girl," capped off with some serious head bobbing. Um hmmm, gimme some!

It seemed 90 percent of the attendees were feeling the same contradiction, yet no one spoke of their deep desire or their fear that love hurts in such a direct, clear manner. Kudos to Patti for being the catalyst and sharing her honest emotions in a hi-frequency format.

Breaking down and identifying the bare bones of Patti's BIG BUT Syndrome® looks a little something-like:

Patti's Desire: *"Wanting love"*

Patti's BIG BUT: *"Opposes her desire for love"*

Patti's Belief: *"Fear of getting hurt"*

Like scores of people, Patti has a considerable desire to fall madly in love, coupled with a BUT belief that opposes her true emotional desire. Each time our BUT opposes our desire, it cancels out that desire. In other words, the BIG BUT cancels out whatever precedes it in our thoughts, speech, or emotions.

Have you ever been to a tractor pull? Or a better question would be, do you know what a tractor pull is? Growing up in North Carolina, tractor pulls were a permanent fixture at county fairs and such. So were monster truck rallies, car races on dirt tracks, NASCAR, and Sunday go-to-meeting church services where people spoke in tongues and kissed poisonous snakes on the lips. Do snakes have lips? I digress.

In essence, a tractor pull is a glorified game of tug-of-war in which school-aged children are replaced by tons of farm equipment, each piece of enormous machinery attempting to pull the weaker side into a manmade mud hole that could easily swallow the entire cast of *Hee Haw* and *The Beverly Hillbillies* put together.

Imagine two tractors, each with the exact amount of horsepower in their high-powered engines, facing in opposite directions. Both vehicles are equally equipped with gargantuan treaded tires and a sturdy chassis all geared up and ready to go.

We'll call tractor number one Desire. Desire represents Patti's desire to fall madly in love, and it is facing south. Tractor number two is Belief, representing Patti's belief she will get hurt when she finds love; Belief is facing north.

In every decent, honest-to-goodness tractor pull, there is a humble steel chain strategically hooked to the backside of each tractor. This chain is connected in such a manner that it evenly distributes the balance between both vehicles. In this way, no tractor has a jump on the other, and the tractor pull is fair and square. The chain represents the BIG BUT Syndrome®.

Desire (Tractor One) and Belief (Tractor Two) are now in the final moments of preparation before competition. Both Desire and Belief rev their fire-breathing motors in a last-ditch attempt to psych out and intimidate the other. The crowd in the stadium grows restless, probably from too much caffeine.

Two eager pit crews of burly men wearing flannel shirts and leather belts with snazzy sayings engraved on them like, "Hi, I'm Charlie Horse," swarm between the ferocious treaded monsters preparing each for the main event. A referee motions the pit crews to finish their task seconds before he waves the starting flag.

Desire and Belief accelerate against one another as Bubba, the crew leader, hooks up the steel chain, which is capable of effortlessly withstanding up to three tons of force. The anxious crowd in the stadium leaps to its feet, screaming as the referee drops the starting flag in a downward motion—and they're off.

From a bird's-eye view in the stadium, it is a sensory marvel to experience the aroma of diesel fuel smoking from beneath raging machines, hear engines whining, and watch as multi-ton machines buck against one another in a challenge to the finish. Mud flies in every direction.

At full acceleration, both engines scream and grind in a dead heat fury as Desire and Belief jerk and jolt back and forth at an exhausting pace. The steel chain holds the tension between each tractor, rarely, if ever, giving either much slack in any direction.

With mud flying and the crowd roaring, Desire gains a few inches to the south and in a second, Belief has gained a microscopic lead to the north. Desire's engine is howling, its tires gripping the mud to create forward movement.

The steel chain continues to hold the tractor tug-of-war in perfect balance. Desire is able to pull Belief a good three feet in the direction of the foreboding mud hole. And just when the crowd thought Desire was locked in and could do no wrong, Belief hunkered down, scrawling and carving the earth like an electric knife in a Thanksgiving turkey.

Bucking and pulsing forward, Desire and Belief pull against one another for the next ten minutes before the referee calls an end to the non-winning twosome, both covered in mud and exasperated from their efforts. In the end, the crowd is irritated to see Desire and Belief are pretty much sitting in the exact same spot they started, give or take the few inches. Belief has managed to pull Desire closer toward the mud hole.

Technically speaking, neither tractor has won, because neither tractor hit the mud hole. Just the same, it is Belief that has managed to pull Desire a touch closer to the dark, muddy pit. After all their effort, hard work, and exhausting planning, they are both basically back at square one.

Bubba quickly dismantles the unbreakable chain from both vehicles and drops it to the ground, liberating Desire to go any direction it chooses and releasing Belief to freely roam.

It is the nearly invisible, non-threatening chain that binds a person's desire and belief together in the tug-of-war of our mind and emotions. When we make the decision to do so, we disengage from our BIG BUT, and the three-ton steel chain confining us simply drops to the ground, freeing us to desire what we choose to desire and own the beliefs that compliment and harmonize with that desire.

The common denominator holding Patti's desire and belief in gridlock is a simple steel chain called the BIG BUT Syndrome®.

Watching the tractor pull, there is no comparison between the tractors' loud motors and the single thread of chain binding Patti's desire and belief together in a stronghold. However, as powerful as her desire is to fall madly in love, it is her fear—a.k.a. *belief* that—she will get hurt "again" if she falls in love that restricts her desire for love.

The BUT Chain that binds our desires and beliefs is virtually unseen and often unheard, because we think the word BUT, we say the word BUT, and act upon the word BUT so often that it goes unnoticed, unseen, and unheard where our five physical senses are concerned. As in the commotion of the tractor pull, all eyes and ears in the audience are fixated on the tractor of Desire or the tractor of Belief fighting against each other while hardly anyone in the stands pays much attention to the BUT Chain that binds Patti's desire and belief in a contradictory knot.

It is our sixth sense, our emotional sense, that perceives the contradiction in our solar plexus when we desire and fear something in the same breath. It is our **Soul Electricity®** that gingerly tugs at our inner guidance system to remind us in a loving manner that using low-frequency thoughts with low-frequency vocabulary (**Vibratory Vocabulary®**) does not serve our highest desire for good.

When we kill our desires, we are, in essence, killing ourselves. We are pulling ourselves further away from a natural state of being. Our birthright is to create feel-good things through our hi-frequency desires and hi-frequency intellect.

Desire makes the world, the Universe, go round. Our belief or justification that we cannot have what we desire is what stops the desire from creating a manifestation on our behalf. To desire love, financial freedom, or the perfect profession is normal; it is our birthright.

The next time you have a considerable desire for a love relationship, money, or a better career, which tractor will you choose to put hi-frequency fuel into? Will you choose to put your energy into the tractor of Desire *"I want to fall madly in love,"* or will you choose the tractor with an opposing belief to your desire, *"I don't want to get hurt again"*? Or, will you choose both?

You may be saying, "Of course I would put my hi-frequency fuel into my desire." BUT, I'll also bet that when you consciously focus on love, money, or career, you will automatically (and innocently) flip back to your old habits, those low-frequency historical beliefs.

Remember to drop your three-ton BUT Chain so your little red tractor has the free will to travel anywhere its heart desires.

Will you unconsciously pick up the steel chain that opposes your desire and get caught in the mental and emotional tractor pull of life? Or, will you appreciate yourself and bask in the Soul Electricity of your heartfelt desire, ignoring outdated beliefs and the Bubbas of life carrying BUT Chains?

As physically focused awareness, we will always operate from a core desire, and we will always have a belief about that desire. Our greatest victory as human consciousness is to own our core desire with pure belief in perfect unison. This brilliant combustion point of consciousness is complete freedom. In essence, this unison is the heart and soul of evolution moving our planet forward.

Desire is the emotion/feeling we crave.

BUT opposes or cancels desire (steel chain).

Belief is our intellectual thought accepted as true.

The moral of our story is: Don't be a Bubba sporting BUT linkage.

2

Proceed With Caution: BUT Zones Ahead

BIG BUT Zones are subjects we observe silently or aloud that cause us to contradict our desires with opposing beliefs to those desires. For example: "I want to go to my high school reunion, *BUT* first I need to lose 15 pounds." In other words, we talk about our desire for lightness while also talking about and feeling overweight. In essence, we are fence-sitting about body image.

The main areas in which we have a tendency to display consistent contradiction are love, money, and career. Other BUT Zones in which we frequently send mixed signals are:

Body image, health, and weight

Sexuality and sensuality

Family, friends, and co-workers

Traffic or commute

Religion and structured education

Aging, death, and dying

Food (When was the last time you ate something decadent without feeling guilty about it?)

Did I mention family? (There's always some serious BUT action happening in the family department.)

ASK YOURSELF:

1-In which areas do you have the biggest BUT, and why?

2-What is my personal self-talk about the area(s) I chose above?

3-What <u>would</u> I like to hear in my mind?

Just for fun, put on your psychic stopwatch. Pick a BUT Zone topic listed above that you personally have problems with. Once you have chosen your topic, begin talking aloud about that topic, and once you contradict the topic with a negative belief, stop the watch and see how long (or how short) a time you spoke before you were infected with the BIG BUT Syndrome. You might surprise yourself.

For example: Let's say you choose Body Image. How long can you write or speak about your body without verbally, mentally, or emotionally saying, thinking, or feeling bad vibes about the amazing machine and mechanics we call the human body?

Isn't it phenomenal what our bodies do every one hundredth of a second? Our hearts pump blood to keep us going while sending thought waves to every atom, cell, and molecule in the visible *and* invisible worlds on a daily basis—all without our giving it a single thought.

Like everything in life, our bodies respond to our invisible thoughts and feelings about it. They cannot do otherwise. If we send our bodies low-frequency feelings, they will respond back to us in a low-frequency manner. And, when we send our body hi-frequency energy, it responds accordingly, giving us back hi-frequency results.

Think about the weight epidemic in our country at the moment. This may shock you, *BUT*, the weight we are wearing is not a direct result of the food we are eating too much of or the lack of exercise in our lives. The weight we are wearing on our bodies is a result of how we *feel* about the food we're eating and how we *feel* about not getting the exercise. We are spending more time and low-frequency emotion on what we DON'T WANT about our bodies than we spend appreciating the absolute miracles our bodies perform every single second of our lives!

If you're not happy with your body, chances are you're focusing on the problem area and not looking at the dozens, even hundreds, of areas in which your body is functioning perfectly—and looking extraordinary, too. Remember, if you don't like your existing body image, it's a direct result of how you've been feeling about it over time. After years of talking about and pointing out the negative parts of your body, the negative points have become bigger.

My good friend Janice tells me she thinks the weight she feels on her body today is a result of how she felt about her body a few years ago. And the weight she felt on her body a few years ago was due to the way she thought and felt about her body five years earlier than that.

A great illustration of what I'm referring to comes in the form of old photographs. I'm in my 40s now. Any time I see old pictures of myself in my 30s, I gasp in disbelief at how slim and trim I was. Of course at the time the picture was taken, I thought or felt heavier and less attractive than I actually was. Talk about not living in the present moment—duh!

Then, I see pictures of myself in my 20s! What the heck was I thinking back then? Again, in my 20s, I was quick to point out my flaws and shortcomings, and today, standing in my 43-year-old body looking back at me then, I easily recognize my invisible negative thoughts of insecurity and self-criticism that have unconditionally followed me through the years. In other words, my body (as all things do) is simply responding to my low-or hi-frequency thoughts about it.

Take a brief moment to recap your BUT Zone areas in history. It seems the older we get, the more intense our personal BUT Zones become and the harder it is to crawl out from under our conflicted beliefs about ourselves.

3

Symptoms of the BIG BUT Syndrome®

Breaking down the word *disease* simply means there is a dis-ease in the vibration of a subject we have chosen to focus on. When I think about Celine Dion singing her heart out in her Las Vegas show, I feel an easy flow in my thoughts and emotions. As I shift my thoughts and feelings to desperately trying to complete two major deadlines in one afternoon, I feel a distinct DIS-ease within myself.

When we continue this level of dis-ease for long periods of time, it eventually diminishes our quality of life. Over time, we will experience one or more of the following symptoms:

Feeling Tired	Lack of Energy	Jealousy
Indecision	Hurt Feelings	Why Me Syndrome
Frustration	Poor Me Syndrome	Needy, Sucky
Blurry Thinking	The Disease to Please	Feeling Not Good Enough
Irritability	Pessimism	Feeling Not Seen
Over Thinking	Whining	Feeling Not Heard
Creating Chaos	Complaining	Imbalanced Ego
Manipulation	Negative Comparison	Directionless
Self-critical	Critical of Others	Seek Outside Approval
Self-hatred	Self-loathing	Complaining

Emotionally holding on to any of these low-frequency attributes for any amount of time will slow down and eventually stop our heartfelt desires. Getting ourselves trapped in this low-frequency quicksand tricks us into turning our backs on our authentic soul power and hypnotizes us into focusing our attention on what we can physically see and hear in the moment.

Our dreams and desires fall into the dark, grim recesses of the BUT Crack of Life, trapped from the light of our whole soul-self.

If we are not careful, we may habitually fall into a dark cycle of believing the life we are living will not change. When we continue to observe the hardships and shortcomings life unconditionally gives us, we will absolutely attract more of the same. I have not met a person yet who can talk, think, or observe negative thoughts for longer than a few moments without possessing low negative vibrations as a result. Conversely, I have not met anyone who focuses on hi-frequency thoughts or events who lives in consistent poverty.

I realized early on while growing up that there are two dominant personality types. They are:

1. Hi-frequency Personalities = Prosperity Consciousness
2. Lo-frequency Personalities = Poverty Consciousness

I deliberately chose the spelling "Hi" over the traditional spelling of the word "High." As we learn more about how words themselves carry an invisible vibration, we will see *and feel* an elevated vibratory output in some words and a lower, lethargic frequency in others. "Hi" literally looks and feels like an invisible, rapid-fire, effective laser point of focus, whereas "high" spelled traditionally looks and feels physically focused, more real, and more normal. It literally feels like a slower frequency of energy is pulsating from it. The same is true for changing the spelling of "low" to a lighter, more hip vibration of the same word to "lo."

Hi-frequency Personalities see the glass as half full. They are more balanced in their right-brain and left-brain transmissions while moving through life operating from their hearts and self-confidence, and standing in the light of their crown chakra. In short, Hi-frequency Personalities are multidimensional and multi-sensory, operating in the world through their soul-self while in perfect sync with their physical, human personality.

Lo-frequency Personalities see the glass as half empty. They complain about the quality of the water in the glass, predicting the glass will surely break and the water will disappear to boot! Lo-frequency people are not good problem solvers as much as they are excellent at discovering new problems in their lives and yours, whether you ask them or not.

They are excellent at shining in a crisis without realizing they themselves created the crisis in which to shine. They operate predominately from the left brain and see the world through their physical eyes more often than they allow themselves to dream desires from their whole-soul perspective.

In short, they choose, more often than not, to focus on the problems and shortcomings in their lives. They look at the world through limited vision, without honoring the heart and emotional dreams their souls are whispering to them.

The symptoms our BIG BUTS trap us in are extreme and chaotic, riddled with hi-frequency desires that are body-slammed to the mat by the WWE of opposing beliefs that we cannot have what we want. Over time, our mind and physical body take a beating from a gamut of invisible feelings rampaging through us with the greatest of dis-ease.

Are you mostly hi-frequency or lo-frequency? Perhaps you are a little bit of both. In the next few days, choose to observe as many things as you can that make you feel good. When you are feeling good, put on your thinking C.A.P.

Celebrate and

Appreciate the moments you feel hi frequency. This in turn

Perpetuates more hi-frequency manifestations. Then begin the cycle again!

4

The OVAL Mirror® of Life

Everyone is familiar with the mean old witch in *Snow White*. The witch stands in her huge castle before her magic mirror and recites the famous question, "Mirror, mirror on the wall, who's the fairest of them all?" In the story, until Snow White comes along, the enchanted mirror always reassures the witch that she is, indeed, the fairest.

Ah, to have a magic mirror in the 21st century; how lovely that would be! To feel guilt-free about having our favorite Ben and Jerry's ice cream at midnight and still have the willpower to stand in front of a magic mirror the next morning without staring at ourselves as if alien seedpods took up permanent residence in our bodies. "What thighs?" the mirror might sweetly say.

When observing ourselves in the mirror for longer than a few minutes, why do most of us have a habit of searching for imperfections and flaws like a heat-seeking missile honing in on its doomed target? Why don't we see our beauty?

It seems we have digressed to, "Is my butt too big for these jeans?" instead of looking for the good. And what of the beauty we possess inside? The compassion, kindness, patience—where are those beautiful aspects of the self celebrated? When did we start believing it was more appropriate to talk about our flaws and imperfections rather than our

29

beauty? When did we begin hiding our true light under a bushel and casting pearls to the swine of our negative focus?

How many times have you stood in front of a mirror semi-horrified as you saw your reflection, wanting to scream, "Mirror, mirror on the wall, don't make me fling you down the hall"? I think it is safe to say many of us have mirror drama in our lives. Whether it is blaming ourselves for giving into that midnight ice cream indulgence, not making it to the gym, or cursing our genetics, standing naked in front of a mirror can bring up our lo-frequency personalities, causing us to feel bad about ourselves.

Because of my fascination with human nature versus the mirror, (kinda sounds like a wrestling match, doesn't it?), I have created the OVAL Mirror®.

The OVAL Mirror of life is one of my favorite tools to use in explaining how we manifest the lives we are living. Since childhood, I have believed all humans have a soul and because of our souls, we do not die. I feel all people are born knowing we are souls being human first and humans being spiritual second. I am certain we came from a heaven-like, angelic world that is unconditional love and pure light. From this heavenly state of consciousness, we choose to be born into the earth plane and live a physical experience.

Because all souls are nonphysical energy in action, designed in the Universal God's likeness, we are 100 percent invisible energy. Once we decide to float from nonphysical energy into a human form, our 100 percent invisible consciousness becomes 99.99% nonphysical, leaving the other .01% to live and function in a physical body. In essence, we are invisibly connected to the nonphysical world through hi-frequency umbilical cords from our Human Intuitive Intellect® and to the heart and soul of God Universe.

As with all mirrors, the OVAL Mirror of everlasting life reflects everything that is in it. Other three-dimensional mirrors reflect only our physical personalities. BUT the OVAL Mirror reflects whatever we are vibrating *on an emotional level*. This extraordinary mirror gives back everything we are vibrating 24/7. If we are vibrating lo-frequency emotions, we get back lo-frequency results. As we choose to focus on positive thoughts, feelings, and memories, the OVAL Mirror unconditionally reflects back to us feel-good physical realities.

I believe every soul, in the process of being born, stood before the OVAL Mirror of everlasting life before being physically incarnated. Because we are still connected to our soul's essence, even while living in human bodies, we have unlimited access to the knowledge and energy that is God Universe. I like the idea that God stood with us in front of the OVAL Mirror before we came to Earth. Together, God read with us the engraving on the OVAL Mirror's ornate frame. The frame reads:

> What I feel is what I get.
> When I choose to feel good,
> I receive good things.
> When I choose to feel bad,
> I receive bad things.
> It is always my choice,
> Because...(repeats)

Because the frame is an infinite, eternal symbol, the carved words wrap around the mirror in a manner that caused our soul to read them until the frequency of these words vibrated so high, so fast, and so pure that every cell in our human bodies was framed with the message that our invisible thoughts, invisible feelings, and invisible vibrations created our earthly realities.

Why is the mirror shaped like an oval? So we would remember how we create our lives on earth with the assistance and power of our invisible, nonphysical Soul Self. Simply stated, O.V.A.L. means that whatever:

We	**O**bserve causes us to vibrate. What
We	**V**ibrate
We	**A**ttract. And what we attract
We	**L**ive

Someone once said misery loves company, and we must believe that. As humans, we have a consistent habit of focusing on what we don't want. We talk about what we don't want, how it feels to have what we don't want, and how unfair it is that we are living what we don't want. We spend more time complaining and activating enormous BUTS instead of dreaming and activating enormous DESIRES. The OVAL effect below gives us an idea of how we attracted the life we are living today:

When we	OBSERVE	the Big BUT
We then	VIBRATE	the Big BUT
Then we	ATTRACT	the Big BUT
Finally, we	LIVE	the Big BUT

Take a moment to let this sink in. If you are not living your highest desires, then recognize that you must change your thoughts and feelings—and the sooner the better! When we **choose** a feel-good decision to play with the miraculous power the Universe affords us, we can shift our focus on an internal level to create our external reality. Our old, habitual, lo-frequency thoughts turn into a new consciousness of hi-frequency thoughts and feelings.

When we	OBSERVE	the Solution
We then	VIBRATE	the Solution
Then we	ATTRACT	the Solution
Finally, we	LIVE	the Solution

Each of us has the free will to choose his or her thoughts and feelings. We have free will about what we choose to observe. It has always been our choice. We can choose the old, lo-frequency thoughts, or we can choose the new desires with supportive beliefs to our desires. It is your choice, your decision.

Lo-frequency =

My butt looks big in these jeans.

My lover will not take out the trash.

I am not getting paid what I am worth.

Hi-frequency =

Hey, my jeans still fit!

Isn't it great, Mike has been so busy lately doing what he loves?

I feel like a million bucks today! I think I'll ask for a raise.

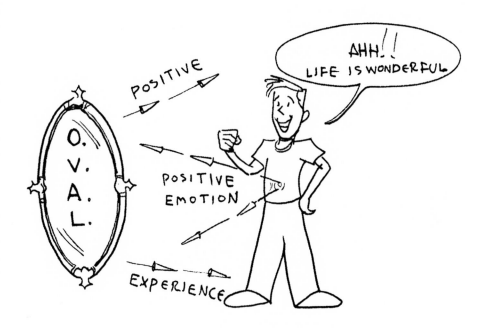

It takes a strong, spiritually centered person to stand in front of a mirror, especially the OVAL Mirror, and make a point to consciously observe his or her positive aspects. To appreciate ourselves unconditionally and applaud our current successes and our future dreams is a gift we can give ourselves. It feels great, and it actually helps us achieve our goals and dreams. It can take extraordinary effort to stand amid the conflicts in your physical life experience and choose to observe beauty in your mind's eye, instead of the dramas being played out around you.

Healing the BIG BUT Syndrome will take some practice. Play with conscious choice and remember the OVAL Mirror of life. Unlock your full human-soul potential by using the God-given gift of Free Will. The free will to choose our thoughts is the greatest present we have in our Present Moment experience. Don't waste it; think a beautiful thought right now!

"Mirror, mirror in my Soul, thanks for making me feel this Whole."

5

The 1-2-3's of Your B-U-T

As your personal BUT Guide, it is my duty to steer you as far away from America's *real* crack problem as I can. By the end of this book, you will be more than able to kick your own BIG BUT. Utilizing the 1-2-3's is a lighthearted way to rise above the BUT habit of having hi-frequency desire with an opposing lo-frequency belief to that desire. Whenever you feel a BIG BUT creeping into your intellectual and emotional awareness, allow the new you to incorporate this simple hi-frequency recipe for success.

B is for Be Aware of the BUT
U is for Undo the BUT Belief
T is for Transcend and Begin Again!

Step1—Be Aware

Be aware of the moments you contradict your desires and beliefs in the same frame of thought. More often than not, out of old, lo-frequency habits, these BUTS slip through the crack of your consciousness, and before you realize it, you are back to the old past-tense aspect of your personality, recycling your old way of thinking and feeling about life.

Being aware that the BIG BUT Syndrome is actively holding your dreams at bay makes you more responsible for allowing your good to manifest. Being conscious that you are using BUT language with BUT emotion does not mean to be self-critical and hard on yourself. It simply means that being aware of your BIG BUT habit NOW will get you closer to living a life filled with ease, not DIS-ease.

Step 2—Undo BUT Beliefs

Undo it. Once you catch yourself being stuck in the trappings of BIG BUT behavior, activate Step 1, **Be Aware**, and immediately implement Step 2, **Undo BUT Beliefs**, with a feel-good frequency. Hi-frequencies always feel good to you. Things like laughing, jokes, humor, music, and affirmations are a few tools to use while undoing this old BUT pattern. The more you feel good, the faster your BIG BUT is defused, leaving you powerfully in the flow of life.

Step 3—Transcend and Begin Again!

Transcend and begin again, utilizing the power and strength of your Soul Electricity. Transcend the normal human belief and go beyond, exceed, and rise above the norm in order to live BUT-Free. This amplifies your desires in a high, pure manner. Transcend your old BUT Belief by reframing your initial BIG BUT statement to fit your hi-frequency desire. Use your Soul Electricity to harness good thoughts, good feelings, and a great outcome.

Choose the power of positive focus. Focus + Feelings = Reality. Reframe, Retrain, and Revive your life by utilizing the 1-2-3's of your B-U-T.

Let's recap Janice's amazing and accurate observation about weight and body image from the BUT *Zones* chapter, while weaving the 1-2-3's of our B-U-T and the OVAL Mirror into a lovely feel-good tapestry. First, we'll reassess our OVAL acronym with: Whatever we

Observe in life causes us to

Vibrate. What we vibrate causes us to

Attract and what we attract, we will

Live.

This OVAL Mirror is an invisible hi-frequency mirror responding and reflecting our thoughts and feelings back to us. For example: if we don't like our bodies in our 20s, this thought and vibration is reflected back to us over the years until it manifests on our person. If we feel ten pounds heavier than we'd like, we are observing a problem that makes us feel bad.

As we observe lo-frequency problems that make us feel bad, we are in that exact one hundredth of a second vibrating, attracting, and eventually living the problem we are observing. And this invisible cycle continues for eternity.

Though I was slightly self-critical of my body in my 20s and 30s, it is easy to see how I created (along with much of the nation) half a lifetime of lo-frequency attributes about body image, and today, I AM living the base of that vibration. In other words, my weight is roughly ten pounds up and down depending on my feelings, or vibratory output.

Today, when I sense those old familiar thoughts and feelings creeping into my awareness, I implement **Step One** and I choose to **Be Aware** that I'm riding out a BUT wave of negativity.

I take responsibility for thinking thoughts like, "I always feel ten pounds heavier than I want to be." By taking responsibility, I am not blaming the ice cream or the hamburger with fries with a chocolate shake and side salad with fat-free dressing. The last time I checked in with myself, these food items have never jumped off the table and into my mouth without my consent. Well, except for that one time on a cruise ship during the midnight dessert buffet. And trust me when I say it wasn't a pretty picture!

I literally stop and **Become Aware** that I am vibrating a contradicted desire that is lo-frequency and springboard into **Step Two and Undo** the **BUT Belief.**

Undoing the old belief is easier to achieve when you employ what I call your Soul Electric attributes. Soul Electricity is always something that makes you feel like a million bucks! And each moment you choose to feel great, you are no longer radiating a contradicted signal that is sabotaging you.

Awareness is a powerful thing. Now that you are aware your hi-frequency thoughts and feelings in the OVAL Mirror of life can change your experience simply by observing feel-good subjects, you will likely loose that old five (or ten) pounds of lo-frequency momentum that you're wearing on your body more easily.

Today, if I accidentally fall into a BIG BUT sinkhole, I immediately begin observing things around me that are working brilliantly on my behalf. I appreciate my home, the houseplants, the flower gardens, the horses, the sunny California weather, talking with mom, my clean and organized office, the hummingbirds outside my window, or the fact that my car starts each time I crank it. And if that doesn't feel like quite enough, I play my favorite music and dance around my house like a big ol' fool! *She's a maniac, maniac on the floor*...I love the movie *Flashdance*—and the soundtrack too!

These are hi-frequency attributes that empower me into being aware and undoing my BUT Beliefs. And now, you are ready to dive head first into Step 3—

Transcend and Begin Again. One of my favorite spiritual principles is that our Focus + Feelings = Reality. It's an abbreviated OVAL Mirror effect.

It feels wonderful to me that my focused thoughts and feelings (invisible attributes) create my physical reality every second of my life. As a result of this basic lesson, I make a deliberate decision to direct my focus toward everything physical and invisible that feels hi-frequency and fabulous to me.

Speaking of body image, another preferred thing I do while I am out and about in the world is to appreciate people with great bodies. Men and women who are toned, slim, trim, muscular, in shape, confident, comfortable, and at ease in their bodies—especially as they move through their day sporting their flattering wardrobe. I use this appreciation technique as my daily *"Feel Good Free-For-All"* ritual. Do this some time. It truly works.

It feels good to feel good! Any moment we choose the luxury and gift of feeling good, we are living—in that exact moment—a BUT-Free existence. Truth be told, that is all we want anyway, isn't it? We want our desires to come to us without the negative backlash we've created for ourselves in the past. Granted, we created the negativity unconsciously with our BUT vocabulary and BUT beliefs, and today, we can start fresh in the *NOW*.

I encourage you to change your life by changing your focus. Choose hi-frequency Soul Electricity over your old programming. Live in the present moment and allow the gift your NOW experience brings to you. And when the BIG BUT sneaks through the cracks of your consciousness, joyously apply a teeny weenie 1-2-3 and blast your B-U-T into orbit.

6

The Truth about Yeah, BUTS

Can I just say that I love Chellie Campbell? For the last 257 days I have carried her book, *The Wealthy Spirit: Daily Affirmations for Financial Stress Reduction* with me all across the country, and I tell everyone about her book. How do I know it has been 257 days? Because her book is broken down into three segments per day: first is the quote, second is a simple story, and third is a daily affirmation that marries the quote and story together. Simply stated, you read one page a day and practice the affirmations for ten minutes. In a sense, each page is an absolute Energetic Multiple Orgasmic Combustion Point (refer to BUT Blaster Nine), and I am grateful to my friend Ellen Dostal for suggesting it to me. Thanks, girl!

I was co-facilitating a retreat in Grand Rapids, Michigan with Mike and Ramona Mucciolo, when I read page 38. It was entitled "Yeah, Buts." The moment I read the title, I gasped aloud.

The chapter illustrates how damaging "yeah, buts" are to ourselves and to the people who offer to help us solve problems in our careers and personal lives. Chellie writes, "'Yeah buts' have a very negative psychological effect on the person trying to help. They've just been rejected, essentially told that their advice is no good, inappropriate, or doesn't work."

43

She continues with, "You will find yourself getting richer and happier when you eliminate the words 'yeah, but' from your vocabulary. Instead of 'Yeah, but' say, 'Thank you for the suggestion! Help me see how I can apply that to my situation.'"

I was also thrilled when I reached chapter 68, which is entitled "Stopping Points." Here, Chellie provides 15 wonderful examples of the "yeah, buts" with easy exercises to rid them from your life.

Yeah, BUTS block our good, suffocate our power, and disillusion us with lo-frequency negativity. When you are spewing "Yeah, BUTS," employ the 1-2-3's of the B-U-T or the AND Avalanches. Call upon the BIG BUT Stand-ins or the Punctuation Shields and if all else fails, utilize my favorite BUT Blaster of all and Laugh your BUT off!

I can honestly say *The Wealthy Spirit* has changed my perspective and given me many new tools to use on my path of spiritual growth and financial stress reduction.

7

The Infamous Invisi-BUTS

"Misery is a communicable disease."

—*Martha Graham*

Invisible BUTS are silent killers surrounding us like ghosts we cannot see or hear. We can only sense these invisible contradictions of energy influencing us deeper and deeper still into the dark crevices of the lo-frequency disconnection from our Soul Self.

The obvious BUTS are the ones we think, speak, and take action toward. We hear ourselves using BUT Vocabulary, and more often than not, we are pretty much conscious of our basic emotional belief about areas that are important to us. Actually, we are so conditioned to using the standard BUT in our thoughts and spoken word that we do not pay much attention to feeling bad when we do utilize the "B" word.

Why have we conditioned ourselves to think it is normal to feel bad and habitually focus on negative, lo-frequency thoughts and things?

Invisible BUTS are sneaky. They do not fight fair, and they love hitting us below the belt.

Invisi-BUTS travel in packs with the intention of penetrating one small, negative belief inside us first, then releasing the rabid pack of BUTS on us next, each one ripping our desires to shreds. Before we know it, we are surrounded by numerous ghosts biting us with lo-frequency fangs over and over until we begin to believe we cannot have our deserved desires.

A typical lo-frequency BUT Belief is: "I need more money, *BUT* I don't know how else to get it."

I met Karen Moriuchi while touring in Hawaii. She is an amazing teacher and an exceptional guide with endless knowledge about the Big Island's folklore and history. Between sights, Karen and I were semi-attacked by wild cocks and frightened by a bearded hermit wielding motorized farm equipment. We nicknamed him The Hawaiian Chainsaw Massacre as we laughed and ran for our lives from chain-saws and wild cocks. *BUT* that's another story for another time.

A master practitioner of NeuroLinguistic Programming (NLP), Karen taught me that BUT is an eraser word. Karen said, "Our brain negates and does not consider what we said before the BUT. I think our brain hears the BUT and then it does not pay attention to what came before it because the information after it is usually contradic-tory…so the brain drops one part of our thought."

In the illustration above, the word BUT erases the desire for money and puts the emphasis on the opposing belief to our "now erased" desire! All the weight now lands on the second half of the sentence, which is the lo-frequency belief, "I don't know how else to get it."

The BIG BUT Breakdown happens when we talk about our desires and BUT beliefs in the same sentence. Desires + BUT Beliefs

= zero results. The desire is erased, and the BUT stands next to our negative belief. Before we realize it, our BIG BUT has taken the bride-zilla of negative belief. That is one honeymoon I don't want to visualize. Yikes.

Unlike their more obvious, outspoken cousin, Invisi-BUTS seem to come from out of nowhere. Using the same category of money, the invisible BUT would take a quiet, silent approach. Here's an example: You're excited because it is payday, and you're ready for a long weekend away from work. You receive your paycheck and swiftly deposit it into the bank, keeping $40 cash for the weekend.

After work, you drive home, check your mailbox, and see them waiting for you. The bills, bills, and more bills piled up in your mailbox, face down, patiently waiting to surprise you. Without warning, your appreciation for your paycheck and the cash in your pocket quickly disappears into the pang of negative emotion in your solar plexus. Suddenly, you believe you have more money going out than coming in. Now, worry has set in, followed by an army of negative, lo-frequency thoughts like, "How am I ever going to get out of this financial mess," or, "I have to find another area to cut back in until I get my credit cards paid off."

Before we realize it, every dollar in our pocket is not nearly enough to get us out of financial trouble. Then we forget to appreciate the gift of the money we possess and instead replace our appreciation of the money we have with the worry-zilla-itis!

Once the first Invisi-BUT penetrates our thin shield, it opens the door to swarms of negative thought patterns that put us in a self-inflicted cocoon of lo-frequency crap. And that's not pretty.

To prevent Invisi-BUT infestation, you want to choose to observe things that uplift, nurture, and serve you. You want to think the thoughts and dream the dreams that enhance your visions and aspirations.

When you feel a lo-frequency pang of negative feeling creeping into your Solar Plexus Megaphone,

STOP and shift that lo-frequency into something higher and more electric that truly honors your new mission statement to win in the game of life,

AND to feel good about feeling good,

AND to share that overflowing wellness with yourself,

AND others around you as frequently as you can.

8

BIG BUT Understudies and Stand-ins on the Stage of Life

Everything has a family of energetic thought associated with it, and our teeny weenie BUT is no exception. Everything seen and unseen has an electromagnetic energy that supports and sustains it.

The more attention we give something, the stronger its lifespan. And the measure of influence we give it always affects our lives in a positive or negative manner. If we give attention to a negative thought, it will affect our lives negatively. BUT, if we give attention to a positive thought, our lives will be affected positively.

By attention, I am referring to thought, emotion, imagination, worry, concern, action, belief, and desire—especially contradicted desire.

Surely all BUTs must need a break from time to time from this production we call life. It is a full-time job for one BUT to run around opposing nearly every desire we have from morning to night, since the first day we were born.

When our overworked BUT finally gets a break from its exhausting show business schedule we call life, it calls on a handful of temporary replacements, or stand-ins (i.e., synonyms) that wait patiently in the wings for their big break in the spotlight.

As the BIG BUT Syndrome® exits the stage of our daily life from sheer exasperation, or takes a vacation from its duties, it summons one of its understudies to step out in its place. These temporary stand-ins will hold down the fort until our BUT steps back in, stealing the show from its less effective apprentices.

Who are these struggling BIG BUT wannabes, desperately waiting in the wings for their big chance in the spotlight? They are none other than the infamous BIG BUT synonyms:

However	Still	Instead
Yet	Nevertheless	

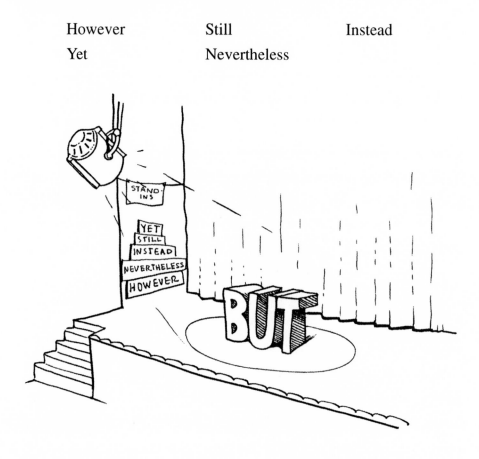

BUT Synonyms introduce, to varying degrees, a statement in opposition to what precedes them. All Big BUT vocabulary has a watered-down, low frequency about it. This includes the less visible apprentices listed above. BIG BUTS are contradicted thought patterns that originate in our conscious thinking, then are immediately packed away into the storehouse of our subconscious mind where they live forever. Our BIG BUTS are seen as smart, physical safety nets designed to caution us from repeating old, familiar patterns or from getting our feelings hurt again.

Not getting overly excited about important matters and being careful not to dream bigger than our means has become one of the most irresponsible habits we, as adults, have fallen into. Somewhere along life's journey, we slowly begin to believe certain people who encouraged us to dream only as high as our credit card limits. These are the same people who taught us that worrying about money, love, or career was responsible adult behavior. In essence, worrying about anything that causes us to feel negative emotion only brings us more things in life to feel negative emotion about. In other words, worrying is NOT a responsible adult act.

Desiring and believing we have the ability to create whatever we want is a Universal Truth. It is an unspoken reality gifted from our Soul Self to our Human Self that lives inside every cell, atom, and molecule of our being that we brought with us when we were born.

We are Souls first and humans second. We choose to come from the nonphysical expression of our being and into a physical body. Upon arriving on Earth in these bodies, we begin expressing our pure Human Soul potential. We are literally Universal Oneness in physical human form. We have the unlimited, unconditional love, guidance, and support from the Universe to experience greatness for ourselves and help others experience their greatness.

When we reach deep in our hearts, we can feel an eager, enthusiastic, animated, electric, brilliant, innocent, all-knowing, loving, and spiritually prosperous genius that has a unique gift to share with the world. All of us are born feeling and knowing our true attributes. Nothing can stop our ability to co-create with the Universe on the behalf of our desires, except us.

The only thing standing between our desires is OUR OWN self-inflicted BIG BUT Belief that we cannot have our desires fulfilled.

Each BUT Stand-In belongs to lo-frequency vocabularies that evoke lo-frequency feelings that will create lo-frequency manifestations. There is no **Soul Electricity** or high, pure frequency within the walls of these words. These words are vibratory family members of our BIG BUT. Our BIG BUT Stand-ins live under the umbrella of the BUT.

A shining example of *Stand-Ins* comes to mind in the guise of a lovely lady I've affectionately nicknamed Ms. Hills. Beverly Hills that is, swimming pools, movie stars. Can't you hear the 70s sitcom music twanging away in your subconscious as the distinguished male commentator announces the arrival of The Beverly Hillbillies in television sets in living rooms across the country?

The Soul Mate Class was held in Los Angeles and was filled with enthusiastic, eager people, hungry to learn new tools for attracting a life partner. I tenderly called this bunch The Rowdy Group, as everyone in attendance was revved up and excited to release their BUT Blocks and attract a relationship. This was an unusually vocal gathering of spiritual people, which is one of my favorite kinds of interactive learning environments.

During this class, Ms. Hills (we'll call her Beverly), a mature lady dripping with emeralds and diamonds and wearing designer sportswear, spoke through her pinched lips and way-too-tight facelift while looking down the slope of her brand-new nose at the other attendees. Beverly fit the image the media paint of wealthy, sophisticated women living in the fabulous 90210 zip code. I liked Beverly instantly and was secretly hoping she would experience a profound breakthrough during our next three hours together.

Beverly, a somewhat nervous and shy person, sat right next to everyone's favorite personality, Patti. Patti was energetic and humorous. You will recall Patti as the *"I do want to fall madly in love again BUT, I'm afraid of getting hurt"* lady from earlier.

After discussing a series of examples of the pitfalls of having a Big BUT and how every one of us verbally or emotionally BUT ourselves dozens of time each day, Beverly glamorously raised her hand with movie star etiquette. "Eddie," she began, "I never use the word BUT while conversing with associates; therefore, I do not have a BIG BUT!"

A potpourri of expressions flashed across people's faces as they considered Beverly's statement. Some rolled their eyes in disbelief, while others searched their brains to figure out if they themselves had ever used BUT in their vocabulary. A small handful of saucy personalities folded their arms in a playful gimme-a-break attitude.

Beverly sat next to Patti near the back of the room. Because of the room's layout and the structure of the chairs, Beverly did not see others rolling their eyes. She continued gazing in the group's direction, seeing through them instead of looking at them. Her animated gestures caused her fingers to dance together like fairy wands ordained with precious emeralds, as if attempting to hypnotize us with the 90210 power of bling-bling.

Beverly resumed, "When my friends and I have the urge to use the word BUT in a sentence, we actually use a more sophisticated vernacular." Having everyone's attention, she proceed, "For example, we'll say the words 'however' or 'still' instead of the word BUT."

In that instant, she became entranced by her own rings and shimmering bracelets. I was excited that Beverly's offering was segueing into the next class segment of *BUT Stand-ins*. I asked her if she would mind sharing a couple of examples with our group. Pleased with herself, Beverly stated, "I have plenty of money; *however*, money can't buy me happiness."

She managed a faint smile while realizing for the first time what she was saying aloud. She attempted another approach, "I have everything I ever wanted, *still* I feel something is missing from my life."

Without skipping a beat, Patti turned in her chair to face Beverly and asked her, "Would that something you are missing just happen to be a man to share your life with?"

Everyone sensed the emotional brakes screeching to an abrupt halt in Beverly's gut. Beverly inhaled a deep, slow breath while addressing Patti, "I am open to having a relationship, if that's what you're asking?"

"It is!" Patti replied warmly, aware her question had evoked a level of vulnerability Beverly was probably uncomfortable expressing in public. Sensing that vulnerability, Patti instinctively reached over and gently touched Beverly's elbow, her eyes warm with genuine affection for her classmate's private sadness.

"Me too," Patti offered. "I'm looking for love, too," she added, taking the extra moment to really see Beverly's contradicted desire and BIG BUT without judgment.

Mike, a burly, 250-pound quarterback riddled with testosterone, sat quietly in the middle of the class in a sea of women. Upon observing the interaction from beginning to end, he announced in his booming, baritone voice, "Hell, I'm looking for love, too!"

After a millisecond of delayed response, the entire group exploded with laughter and sincere smiles. Within seconds, all were basking in one wave of enlightenment after the other.

I appreciated Beverly's efforts to detach from her BIG BUT with BUT Stand-Ins, *BUT* there was still a solid contradiction woven in the emotional fabric of her sentences and her desires.

The words BUT, *However, Still, Yet, Nevertheless,* and *Instead* vibrate the same and function the same, regardless of how we use them. To demonstrate this case in point, I wrote the following sentences on the board for our group while replacing the word BUT with *BIG BUT Stand-ins*:

I crave love; HOWEVER, I don't want to get hurt.

I crave love; STILL, I don't want to get hurt.

I crave love; YET, I don't want to get hurt.

I crave love; NEVERTHELESS, I don't want to get hurt.

I crave love INSTEAD of hurt.

Our group agreed the *Stand-Ins* looked and sounded different than the word BUT, and in true energetic form, each *BUT Stand-in* basically felt the same in our gut. Ultimately, the Big BUT is the star and headlining act when it comes to contradicted desire in our lives. Whichever word we choose, whether it's the big cheese or a temporary stand-in, each word functions in complete association with the headliner. Stars and stand-ins alike oppose our desire, cancel our desire, or erase our desire all together, leaving the power of our old BUT belief standing in the spotlight alone.

Over the years, I have learned it is NOT the word that creates; it is how we vibrate while using the word that causes the creation. The higher the word's vibration takes us, the greater our physical results will be.

9

Riding the AND Avalanche

While facilitating BIG BUT Workshops around the country, I ask attendees to finish the following sentence: "I really do want a relationship, BUT…" My pattern with this exercise is to ask the question with machinegun repetition and point to a new person each time I repeat it. The objective is to assist people in becoming familiar with their desires instead of their contradicted desires. The following is a list of answers to the infamous question, "I really do want a relationship BUT…"

"BUT I don't want another jerk."

"BUT not if they don't have a decent job."

"BUT I don't want to get hurt."

"BUT I don't want history to repeat itself."

"BUT I don't want to waste my time."

"BUT I'm afraid to commit to one person."

"BUT I don't want to pay another man's bills."

"BUT I don't have time to baby sit."

"BUT I would rather be happy and single than in a relationship and miserable."

It was interesting to hear everyone's innate response to the question and fascinating to witness the similarities among the group. Though every response was different, you will notice each has a lo-frequency feeling that contradicted each person's desire for love.

Mass conscious belief is an extraordinary phenomenon. It is also hard to buck when we are not feeling completely on our game. Meaning, when we feel lo-frequency emotions for a long period of time about subject matter important to us, we will attract people, places, circumstances, and situations that promote and solidify our worst suspicions. In this case, the suspected belief is that love hurts.

The same is true, of course, of our best suspicions. Isn't it interesting to be in a human body while having complete access to the knowledge and wisdom of the Universe's heart and soul? More interesting still is that we often forget this gift is available to us. I believe the greater collective consciousness holds that on a core level, everything is operating like a well-oiled machine in perfect synchronicity with our higher, spiritual desire.

Our eager group conversed about our emotional discoveries around the "I really do want a relationship BUT" exercise, then together, we began a new approach.

With the next exercise, the stipulation was that their answers had to focus on their *DO WANTs* instead of their *DO NOT WANTs*. Sounds simple, right?

I asked a new person the exact same question three times in a row, hoping to find someone who could answer it without hesitation or contradiction. It is fun to ask this question in rapid-fire succession, one right after the other. You can literally see and feel each person called upon searching in the deepest archives of their subconscious mind while frantically reaching for a DO WANT answer.

The following answers are honest and true accounts from real people. Again, the new question was: "I really do want a relationship AND…"

"AND…ugh…umm…I dunno?"

"AND I don't want to get hurt as badly as before."

"AND you're joking right?"

"AND uh, what she said."

"AND oh my goodness, I'm clueless."

"AND I do want a relationship."

"AND…this is a trick question isn't it?"

"AND I want it to feel good. Can I ask for that?"

Their eyes grew to the size of saucers—flying saucers. Pauses, hesitation, and nervous energy complete with hand and arm movement abounded in our group. When I first began teaching BIG BUT 101, I was surprised how hard it was for most people to openly discuss their much-deserved desires.

I have spent as much as 15 to 30 minutes on this exercise during workshops alone, as much time as it takes until one brave person takes a leap of faith from their existing programming and blurts three answers to the question aloud.

This example shows how our outdated responses are ingrained systems of thought that rattle to the forefront of our conscious mind, causing our mouths to automatically spew lo-frequency data that negate our heartfelt desires. It is a habit to observe the lo-frequency attributes around us. The real world—what we can easily see, touch, taste, hear, and smell—is considered a healthy approach. What about all the invisible frequencies that attracted our current circumstances and physical manifestations to us?

I believe we must look at our human soul personality as the multi-dimensional energy it is and take a new action that is purely inspired with the intention of our Intuitive Intellect or Universal Mind to back us up. Because most people had difficulty asking aloud for their desires, I created the **AND** *Avalanche*.

AND *Avalanches* are bridging tools that wean people from BIG BUT Dis-ease and put them one thought and feeling at a time into their desires with little or no opposing belief to those desires. AND Avalanches promote one AND after the next, after the next, and after the next in fast repetition until we get used to *thinking* our desires in a format. The AND Avalanche is designed to replace the rickety old BUT shanty of our former beliefs and replace it with a new, solid foundation that supports our current dreams, goals, and aspirations.

How many AND Avalanches can you come up with? Create a list here for the desires you want to manifest in the area of love-life, financial freedom, or career. Take 60 seconds for this while coming up with as many AND Avalanches as you can. Good luck.

List your desired subject with AND Avalanches here:

1-	6-
2-	7-
3-	8-
4-	9-
5-	10-

The following is an example of an AND Avalanche. Once the group gets going on a positive free-for-all, there is no stopping the stampeding positive emotion pouring forth. We had a ton of fun creating this list, and I have confidence you will enjoy it as well. Avalanches away!

I desire a wonderful marriage

AND I want it to be with my life mate

AND I know it will feel easy and fluid

AND I can feel it will be a win-win partnership

AND I really want to laugh my BIG BUT off with it

AND I know it will be sexy, sensual, and delicious

AND I want to appreciate, adore, and love him/her

AND I want to appreciate, adore, and love myself

AND I want it to have an element of pleasant surprises

AND I want to focus on his/her positive attributes

AND I want us to be the best we can be

AND I want us to live this essence in the OVAL Mirror of life!

Using *AND* Avalanche Alternatives

And	With	That	Plus
Along with	Together with	As well as	
Also	In addition to	Including	

Using the SOUL-ution consciousness of the AND Avalanche Alternatives, your itty bitty, teeny weenie BUT can finally take its much-needed vacation back to the dictionary of tropical getaways so your Avalanche Alternatives can shine on the sturdy stage of your new desires. Joyously give these Alternatives the spotlight and center stage of your consciousness, allowing them to bask in one standing ovation vibration after another. Allow the lovely audience of your desires the glorious pleasure of appreciating you. Give this desire and belief permission to join in soul harmony and shout more, more, and more as the Universe answers one desire after the next.

Yippee!

On that note, bring your dreams, goals, and aspirations into the spotlight as they embrace the AND Alternatives. Open your mind and feelings for an energy-focusing game.

Please complete the following sentences while utilizing AND Alternatives to escalate the momentum of your wishes. Enjoy yourself, and truly have fun stretching from your old, past-tense, lo-frequency beliefs into vibrating in your new, present-moment attitudes.

"I clearly wish for an amazing relationship"

WITH_____

AND_____

THAT_____

Focusing on the subject of money, let's repeat the exercise.

"I desire a lifestyle that promotes consistent financial freedom"
ALONG WITH_____
TOGETHER WITH_____
AS WELL AS_____

Lastly, we focus attention on the subject of career or life purpose.
"I want a new career in which I am paid big bucks for being myself..."
ALSO _____
IN ADDITION TO_____
INCLUDING_____
PLUS_____

It feels good to know you are in the process of bringing outdated thought patterns to the forefront and replenishing your conscious and subconscious mind with **Vibratory Vocabulary**® that supports you. As we practice these techniques frequently throughout the day in our mind, speech, thoughts, journals, writing, self-relationships, actions, and feelings, our physical lives will begin to reflect our invisible attitudes into physical creations.

In November 2002, David Ault introduced me to John Livesay. John is the West Coast Director for *W* magazine. At the time, David was in the home stretch of his first book, *Where Regret Cannot Find Me*, which piqued John's enthusiasm to move forward with his own writing. John wanted to create a book to demonstrate his successful selling secrets with passion and integrity.

John took what my friend and Coach Melissa McFarland calls "Inspired Action" to produce his book. He set out to complete his writing in a relatively short amount of time, given his full-time responsibility at *W*. He had a vision and strong desire, and he worked hard. John walked the talk his book would illustrate, thus turning his idea into an amazing reality.

In January 2004, David invited me to John's book launch party in Bel Air. I knew this was an unprecedented opportunity to practice the power of the **AND Avalanche** and the **TAGS Technique** (BUT Blaster One), so off we went.

We arrived excited. The valet took David's car, then escorted us to a shuttle that climbed the half-mile driveway to a private home that was to die for. Celebrities maneuvered the red carpet and bright lights as dozens of paparazzi snapped pictures with the man of the hour and his famous guests.

John greeted us with warm hugs and led us to the red carpet to have our pictures taken with him. His eyes twinkled with excitement as handlers guided him from one important element of the party to the next.

Once inside the stately home, appreciative guests were surrounded by live music, jaw-dropping art, stunning esthetics, gorgeous design, fabulous fountains, brilliant swimming pools, decadent food and beverage, a perfect moonlit night, breathtaking views of the Los Angeles skyline, and a atmosphere abundant with grateful people celebrating one man's success. It was effortless to love the guests, AND the essence of the gathering, AND teenagers playing classical music, AND the cake. I can't believe I forgot the cake!

From the beginning of the evening to the very end, every aspect of John's function ran like universal clockwork. It was fun *TAGGING* beautiful things and interesting people, and observing John's success.

While maneuvering through the party, I had the realization that each of us gathered was a co-creator in John's intention. I couldn't help but realize that John must have had numerous visualizations about this event long before it occurred. This led me to recognize something important: that our big dreams do not have BIG BUTS. We do. Our Soul or Higher Self never has contradicted energy. We do.

As physical consciousness, we are more invisible than we were taught to believe. Belief itself is an invisible reality. We must first hold the essential electricity of the invisible belief inside us purely before we can physically produce the basis of the belief. We were trained out of our nonphysical attributes and trained to be seers of the material world.

In that instant, I had greater appreciation for the power of visualization with pure desire. I adore creative personality types and more than that, I love to see what they manifest for themselves. I enjoy conversing with creative people about their creation techniques, their envisioned goals, and how they will produce their burning desires.

John created a masterpiece based on his invisible desire and strong belief to create his first book, *The 7 Most Powerful Selling Secrets: Soar Your Way to Success with Integrity, Passion and Joy.* Even the title is imbued with energy.

Use AND Avalanches every opportunity you have. Doing so raises your vibratory output, uplifts your emotional frequency, and magnetizes your good toward you even faster. Not to mention the fact that it centers you deeper into the heart of Appreciation.

10

Super Hero Punctuation Shields—BUT Armor

To write down our invisible thoughts, ideas, or emotions is an extraordinary way to pull our nonphysical attributes into physical manifestation. It is also a fun NEW way to break the Past Tense belief patterns that no longer serve us today in our Present Moment experience.

This is a great exercise to play with. It is also a predominately left-brain focused tool that feels good creatively.

The fastest way to stop a rampant BUT dead in its tracks is by the use any of the following devices. You guessed it, never underestimate the power of punctuation.

Any person can become a kick BUT superhero with the following ammunition. Okay, put away those Wonder Woman bulletproof bracelets and Xena breastplates, and get ready to replace them with the BIG BUT Punctuation Shields. Get ready, set, and fire the ever-popular and highly underestimated Period, Exclamation Point, and Comma. The words AND, WITH, and THAT provide additional ammunition.

This turns our once-contradicted desire into a clearly focused vibratory intention. Once again, our amazing class read aloud each sentence using their new BUT Armor. With each sentence, we held our hands softly over our solar plexus "stomach area" so our class could feel the difference in the vibration of the vocabulary and punctuation. Reading aloud as a group, the enthusiasm grew and the energy radiated higher. By the time we read the last sentence, the entire gathering felt uplifted about their new, non-contradicted declarations; even Beverly, Hills that is.

I desire love.   I desire love!   I desire love, hppiness, *and* joy.
I desire love AND happiness!
I desire love WITH a win-win partner.
I desire love THAT amplifies my positive strengths and attributes.

It was good to see and experience everyone coming to life with a soulful articulation of their desires. This practice begins eliminating the Past Tense "Old Historical Patterns" of thinking and believing and begins to RE-build toward our desired reality. Practicing this technique over time puts a new concrete foundation in place NOW, today, so that when we do step into our future, our new foundation of desire is strong, sturdy, consistent, and REAL-istic.

We can believe we can have love that is uplifting and a bank account filled with money and the freedom it brings. It starts with a single, pure thought that carries a vibration.

Each NEW in the NOW thought vibrates our outdated BUT Beliefs deeper into the hibernating caves to sleep in the winter of our historical programming. Meanwhile, our new Present Moment Personality is building a solid foundation into the structure of our new life filled with an abundance of love, money, career, and much more.

Congratulations in advance for appreciating yourself and building bridges to your New in the NOW Empire of Desire.

Section Two:
The SOUL*ution*

11

Twelve BUT BLASTERS— Soul Tools to Obliterate Your BIG BUT

BUT Blasters are hi-frequency solutions that minimize our BIG BUTS. When we flip the word solution into a hi-frequency Vibratory Vocabulary®, we get **SOUL**ution. Our Soul is a pure, nonphysical expression of the unconditional love that guides and supports us in life.

Making a conscious choice to focus on one or more of these hi-frequency tools can vaporize your big-ass BUT into kingdom come.

Before you realize it, your old manner of observing the world will gradually melt away a little at a time, and all of a sudden, your new perspective becomes the familiar norm. Each moment you feel genuine good pouring through your mind, heart, and emotions, you are light years closer to living your full human-soul purpose.

Adults not only have BIG BUTS, we focus on our BUTS more than necessary, whereas our Spirit, Soul, and God Essence doesn't have a BIG BUT at all. (Good Lord, can you imagine for just a second what the world would be like today if God Universe had a Big BUT!?) "I'd like to let you into my pearly gates, Donald Trump, *BUT* you're fired!" Our invisible attributes are pure Universal Energy conspiring to bring our desires to us with great ease. The moment we consistently choose to observe thoughts and feelings that are BUT Free, we will begin living our personal heaven on earth.

The more time we spend in our personal BUT Blaster areas, the faster we can attract our desires and dreams coming true. I believe our dreams and visualizations are a thousand-fold stronger a reality than the physical world we live in. The only difference between our invisible world and our physical world is that we usually spend 90% more time in our physical world (what we can see and hear) while we spend less than 10% of our time and energy holding the pure vision and desire of what we do want in our lives.

Now I'm no mathematical genius, BUT even I can see the scale hugely tipped 90% more in the direction of what is not wanted in this scenario. As a result of this daily dilemma in our lives, I've decided it would be hi-frequency fun to share Twelve BUT Blasters for you to experiment with.

As promised, here are Twelve Spiritual *SOUL*-utions promoting and empowering us to focus on our desire without contradicting that desire with a BIG BUT Belief:

1. The TAGS Technique®
2. Feeling Good
3. Laughter and Humor
4. Nature
5. Music, Tones, and Harmonics
6. Praying with a Pure Heart
7. Intuitive Intellect®
8. Vibratory Vocabulary®

9. Energetic Multiple Orgasmic Combustion Points®
10. Artistic/Creative Expression
11. Visualization and Imagination
12. Daydreams and Night Dreams

ᵖᴸᵁˢ THE ESSENCE of THE SOUL

BUT Blaster One   The TAGS Technique

"If only the people who worry about their liabilities would think about the riches they do possess, they would stop worrying. Would you sell both your eyes for a million dollars...or

your legs...or your hands...or your hearing? Add up what you do have, and you'll find that you won't sell them for all the gold in the world. The best things in life are yours, if you can appreciate yourself."

—*Dale Carnegie*

The TAGS Technique is the easiest and purest form of merging with Universal Consciousness. When we appreciate, we light up like a million stars on a clear night. Appreciation is a clear, laser-like signal of adoration and unconditional love from us to the Universe and back again, creating a full circle of pure desire with pure manifestation of that desire.

Appreciation is a living energy that activates our inner light and our soul knowing. This light and knowing penetrate all time and space reality, as we physically know it to be, and surpasses all worlds to get our signal of appreciation to the powers that be. Thus, appreciation is the most effortless and effective manner in which to communicate with the Universe in a consistent manner so that we may reap heavenly results here on Earth.

It was through utilizing the power of Appreciation that I created a playful tool I call the **TAGS Technique**®. The TAGS Technique employs the principles of:

Thanksgiving

Appreciation

Gratitude and

Sending Soul Signals

And presto, we have **TAGS**®!

Although Thanksgiving, Appreciation, and Gratitude basically mean the same thing, they each feel a touch different from the other. My clients seem to respond to Appreciation and Gratitude over the feeling of Thanksgiving. Or, as my friend Marissa says with noted humor, "Thanksgiving reminds me of food, and food makes me hungry." She's a good little eater. Everyone's different. It is our different beliefs and different desires that make the world an extraordinary place to live.

I can honestly say it is easy to find something every hour that I am thankful for, that I appreciate, or that makes me feel happy that I am able to continue doing what I love to do for a living.

The power of our feelings is barely seen as a viable catalyst in creating our human reality. I predict you will continue to see a trend in the next ten to twenty years of authors writing and speaking on nothing but the power of our human feelings and emotions. It will be especially exciting when the scientific and medical communities come together and consistently acknowledge that our hi-frequency emotions and lo-frequency emotions create our physical lives. While today the power of feelings still seems unimportant, in the coming years it will be seen as leading-edge thought.

Consciously using the power of Thanksgiving, Appreciation, and Gratitude activates and sends pure, laser-focused **Soul Signals** into the heart and soul of God Universe. The Soul Signals we send to the Universe through the art of the TAGS Technique is just a smidgeon of how we can consciously co-create with our Soul Electricity:

Our Focus + Our Feelings = Our Reality

Our Soul Self is working for us unconditionally, even when we forget to take good care of ourselves. When we forget to look at, think about, or focus on the things in our lives that enhance our personal experience, our Soul Electricity holds a vigil of unconditional love and eternal support.

As the power of our **Soul Electricity**® becomes global knowledge, people will be less likely to contradict their desires and beliefs about love, money, and career and instead will feel empowered to deliberately create miracles in those areas of their lives.

BUT Blaster Two   **Feeling Good**

"First feelings are always the most natural."

—Louis XIV

Feeling Good sounds like more metaphysical woo-woo that's much a-do about nothing, *BUT* don't cross this petite morsel of life-changing material out of your little black book of conscious co-creating the life you want just yet. I have understood the meat and potatoes of feeling good since the age of seven or eight, and I remember it today as if it were yesterday.

The season was fall, my favorite in the Carolinas. Cool sunlight broke through the trees, its light amplifying millions of brightly colored leaves that clung to their homes among the trees surrounding our property. Each caressing breeze animated these treasures of beauty everywhere I looked. The early foliage of ruby reds, amber golds, and cinnamon orange showered past me, escorted by the sound of rustling tree limbs in the afternoon sky as I sat on an oil drum watching my mom hang our family's laundry on the clothesline behind our home.

Mom didn't know I was perched quietly on the 50-gallon drum, mesmerized by the crisp, fresh air and the sound of her singing and humming songs under her breath while she worked. The feeling of peace and goodness in the air that afternoon was transforming and abundant. We didn't have much in the way of physical wealth, but on this afternoon, I was the richest kid in the state.

Mom was always a serious and responsible person who rarely took a break from work or life. She often moved from one household chore or yard project to the next, tired and exhausted to the bone from long shifts in a textile mill, family errands, and our school activities. The hours never stopped her from preparing home-cooked meals, keeping a spotless home, and tending a well-manicured lawn.

Her attention and love were never focused on herself, but on her four boys. Because she was so intent on getting things done with hardly time to breathe between chores and work, it surprised me to hear her singing. When she wasn't singing, she was humming with a pleasant, relaxed expression on her face. I loved seeing my mom in such a feel-good, radiant space.

This day felt like a blessing for everyone it touched. My senses were on pleasant overload watching mom in the amber-golden light, singing softly as she did her chores—chores I realized for the first time were designed to make her kids' lives better and enhance her own life as a good mother.

The moment became fairy-tale like. For an instant, I sensed I was someplace greater than my private oil-drum sanctuary. A surge of energy tickled my solar plexus, delivering a message that covered me with goose bumps. My eyes watered with the rich, hi-frequency message that came from the spirit of the afternoon.

"God Is Good," reverberated in unison through my mind, heart, and solar plexus in perfect sync.

It was not the words that convinced and converted me right there on the oil drum, but the sheer emotional electricity I felt in every cell and molecule in my being. It was a combination of the day and its beauty, of observing my mom as she felt good and allowing myself to slip into the abundance of the moment and experience the complete richness of the afternoon.

Something bigger than the love I felt for Mom happened inside of me that day, something I have carried my whole life.

Every single moment we choose to feel good in life, we choose a higher awareness that harmonizes our invisible dreams, goals, and aspirations into a physical manifestation. When we feel good, and that *God is Good*, we activate our true essence, we create miracles, and we are more likely to live the life we were born to live.

Feeling good, feeling God (or Universe) is a sure BUT Blaster. I love finding new things to feel good about. Give yourself permission to go on a Feeling Good Free-for-all. Find anything and everything in your imagination and physical reality that makes you feel good, gooder, goodest, and GREAT! The longer you experience this hi-frequency goodness coming to you and pouring through you, the faster you successfully pull the goodness in life to you. Have fun and enjoy yourself.

BUT Blaster Three   **Laughter and Humor**

"Before my gratitude journal began, there were things out in the world that I wished never existed, like mosquitoes."

—Ellen Degeneres

Laughter is one of the most healing gifts we possess. There is a reason situation comedies abound on national television, comediennes like Ellen Degeneres have hugely successful shows, and Jim Carrey makes $20 million a movie to make people laugh. Comedy clubs, plays, movies, radio stations, books, magazines, children's games, and even traffic schools have chosen to add fun and amusing twists and turns to their formats. Why? Because they have discovered that when we are feeling good, we get more accomplished. Approaching important tasks from a hi-frequency perspective with tools like humor and laughter facilitates learning difficult tasks easily, increases productivity, and enhances our ability to live a longer, healthier life.

The other day, I heard a comedian on television say his only tool to survive growing up in the New York projects was to get the other kids to laugh at him or to laugh with him. This comic's belief was that if you could get the bullies to laugh with you, they would be less likely to beat the crap out of you.

Laughing is an unpolluted hi-frequency action that raises our vibration and can raise the vibration of others around us. It simply feels good to laugh and feels better when others laugh with us. Laughing erases color lines, prejudices, hurts, heartaches, negative emotions, and blame, to name a few.

Children laugh hundreds of times a day, while adults only laugh an average of five to seventeen times a day. Access that natural comedian/comedienne inside you, the one called your soulful, inner child, and give that animated aspect of you permission to tickle your funny bone. Make a conscious feel-good decision to lock into the aspects of your life that cause you to smile and laugh.

Start with a smile first. Smile with yourself before you leave for work in the morning. Direct your winning smile toward your co-workers and give out genuine healing smiles to people you don't even know. Watch how contagious your smile feels and how a simple smile can raise your energetic vibration and then ripple out to the world.

After a few hours of sharing your smile, you will notice the caliber of person around you begins to change. Smiling often leads to pleasant exchanges of energy with others. Pleasant exchanges of energy lead to humor, and humor leads to laughter. Smiling, humor, and laughter will always create an enormous chain of synchronicity that enhances and enlightens our lives and the lives of others. Go ahead—smile!

Smile from the inside out. Think of something funny that lifts your thoughts to a lighthearted pitch. Can you remember a funny moment from the past that caused you to howl with laughter? A moment when you laughed so hard that the soda you were drinking flew out of your nose like an open fire hydrant valve on a hot summer day? Or a time you and your friends were laughing so hard that neither of you could catch your breath or say a word without starting a whole new avalanche of self-inflicted laughter again? Now that's laughing your BIG BUT off!

Treat yourself and share a smile with someone you love and care about. What better person to share your genuine smile with than YOU!

BUT Blaster Four   **Nature**

> *"All nature wears one Universal grin."*
>
> *—Henry Fielding*

Nature is an entire world of perfection within itself that causes us to believe once and for all that there is something bigger and greater than our elementary human comprehension can grasp. Nature has a rhythm unto itself that humankind has attempted to tap into and duplicate since Adam and Eve.

The most effortless way to tap into nature's majesty is to be in it, appreciate it, and honor it. It is almost impossible to be in nature and not be filled with a sense of goodness and appreciation.

One of my favorite and most influential metaphysical teachers is Abraham-Hicks. Abraham is channeled by a lovely lady from Texas. Each Abraham-Hicks Publication tape comes with a question and answer segment asking simple questions about daily life. Abraham answers their questions strictly from a nonphysical perspective while shining clarity on the stage of our human experience.

It was on a Tape-of-the-Month that I heard Abraham say to the audience, "Have you ever seen a tree worried about paying a mortgage? Do you think the ocean wonders what its property value is these days?" Abraham went on to say that every aspect of nature is tuned in, tapped in, and turned on to the stream of pure, positive energy that creates worlds. When nature asks for something, it allows the Universe to deliver its request.

Trees do not justify their existence; the ocean does not justify its reason for being. Only humans justify and contradict their desires with resistance, aka The BIG BUT Syndrome. We ask the Universe for what we say we want, then we justify why we should have it, why it should have already been here, and then we often blame some other person or thing in our lives as the cause for why we don't have it.

We could learn a lot from the power of nature. When animals ask, they allow. When a tree asks, the tree allows. When the ocean asks, the ocean allows its requested good to come to it. This happens not because the animals, trees, and ocean deserve to have it, but because they simply exist. Nature understands it is worthy and deserving to have what it asks for simply because it exists in perfect harmony with All That Is. When people learn to ask for what they desire without opposing their desires with resistance, they will easily attract the manifestation of their desires.

Nature seems to be the place we run to in an attempt to regain lost balance. Thoughts that have overwhelmed us and internal dialogues that weigh heavy on our hearts seem to melt away as clarity and decision arrive within the majesty of a great forest or on the shores of a brilliant beach rich with treasures, beauty, and connection to our Source.

Nature was a main source of solace for me even before I entered the first grade. Our family moved to the country, to a rural, two-acre spot that bordered cow pastures, sloping hills, and a meandering creek that skirted two sides of our new property.

When things in our household were hectic or overwhelming, I retreated to the thin veil of woods behind our home or to the meadows that nestled the woods and stretched for miles. I loved to lie in the grassy carpet of pasture and watch the sky stretch for all eternity, as my intuition and imagination delivered messages and images of wellness that were sure to come from the adversity and conflict our family was going through at the time. I would often sit on the banks of the creek in a glassy-eyed daze as the minnows, crawdads, snapping turtles, and bullfrogs danced beneath the water's murky surface.

Walking in the woods, sitting in the infamous five-limb tree, or lying in the meadow was my escape from the physical drama in my life and a retreat back to my whole soul-self.

Over time, my conflict and confusion about the whys of life subsided into brilliant balance and conscious clarity. My smile and love of life returned, and my happiness was restored with each abbreviated retreat to the pure, positive energy nature unconditionally provided me.

Desert landscapes and mountain ranges not only deliver us fresh clean air, but a delicious new perspective. It is in nature that we *can* see the forest for the trees and see the light at the end of the tunnel and essentially get out of our own way long enough to savor the hi-frequency healing all around us.

Nature restores and fills us with hi-frequency fuel that we take back to our homes and workplaces. It gifts us with the soul alignment, wholeness, and sense of well-being we lost somewhere during endless errands, carpooling, and frustrating careers in which we are overworked and underappreciated. As a matter of fact, I strongly believe nature saved my mom's life more than once.

As I said earlier, my mom worked nonstop for our family. Endless hours of working her fingers and her spirit to the bone did not slow her down, even when the doctors took half her left lung in 1973 due to a misdiagnosis of tuberculosis. Mom pulled herself back from the depths of a month-long hospital stay to take care of her young'uns. Before we knew it, Mom was back in full force and though she was in great pain, she rarely allowed us to see it.

Mom was on an automatic pilot of never-ending, 18-hour work-days. I rarely saw her sit still for any amount of time, except when our family vacationed at the beach. Mom's transformation from the daily chores and hard work of real life melted away with every breath of salt air she inhaled as we approached the North Carolina coast. The muscles in her face would soften, the tension in her neck and shoulders would subside, and the lovely twinkle in her eyes would return. As we neared the beach, she became more childlike, even giddy, with her eagerness and expectation of what the beach always provided her. And when we could actually see the ocean, her soul-self would return as she dissolved into a deep, peaceful trance of appreciation. Her sense of humor, contagious spirit, and full heart lavished each of us with verbal hugs, and her abundant smiles spoke nonverbal *I love yous* that were priceless.

The beach has always been Mom's favorite place to visit. It makes her feel healed, whole, and healthy again. It restores her spirit and renews her faith that everything will be okay.

In 1997-98 the doctors took the remaining half of Mom's left lung. She was in and out of the hospital between November and January, and almost died three times during her recovery period. It was a scary time for all of us. For a long time after her surgeries, things looked dismal. I have never prayed so much in my lifetime as I did during those four months. Then, the funniest thing happened. In the late spring of 1998, my Aunt Shirlee organized a two-week trip to Myrtle Beach and invited the family to come with her. Mom and I orchestrated our schedules to join my aunt for one week.

Mom still felt the severity of the surgeries for months. With only one lung, her breathing was difficult and more labored. The simplest things in life were huge obstacles to her now. Things like bending over to vacuum or walk the driveway for the daily mail made her life a living hell. As if that wasn't enough, she was having trouble battling the humidity of the North Carolina summers. Just leaving the comfort of her air-conditioned home became an issue. Now, just the thought of going to the ocean soothed and transformed her spirit just as it had when we were children.

I flew in from California and joined Mom, and together we drove to the coast to meet up with Aunt Shirlee. We laughed and girl-talked during the five-hour commute and once again, as we neared the coastline, Mom could smell the salt air, and her metamorphosis quickly began.

We arrived in the early evening with a near full moon that lit the night sky. The moment Mom could hear and see the ocean, heaven was restored again in every cell of her being. In a sense, Mom was home. Her spirit was back in full force. I was relieved.

Early the next day, Mom and most of our extended family walked four miles on the beach. She was energized and happy again. Everyone was relieved to see her physically and emotionally gravitating back to her soul-self. I felt blessed, and I thanked God Universe for answering our prayers.

The attributes nature provides Mom and all of us are priceless. We simply need to remember to take advantage of its infinite possibilities.

When we are not physically out in nature, our Soul brings aspects of nature to us. Domestic pets, houseplants, flowers, water fountains, stones, trees, and materials for landscaping are simple expressions of our connection to the healing energies of the nature kingdom. It's no wonder home improvement centers and pet stores make a killing these days.

In the future, don't wait until you are sick and tired of the same old daily grind of life before you get away to the replenishing, revitalizing elements of nature. Make a heartfelt promise to get outside at least once a week. Getting back to nature can give you the clarity and alignment you deserve.

BUT Blaster Five   Music, Tones and Harmonics

"Music produces a kind of pleasure which human nature cannot do without."

—*Confucius*

Music is an authentic universal language that can completely stop any clock ever made. It transcends time and space reality with its tones, harmonics, and vocals, the whole time raising our vibration and often transporting us back to moments in our past that we had long forgotten.

In the fall of 2002, while riding with my friend Max, he popped a compilation CD into his car stereo. He had made the CD himself, burning all types of music from Broadway, Pop, and Rhythm and Blues, to the Oldies of the 60s and 70s. When the song "Downtown" came through the speakers of Max's car stereo, my mind and emotions immediately recaptured a forgotten moment from my youth. It was a time in my childhood when my mom listened to high-energy songs on her car radio while running errands with us kids.

I remembered the first time I heard "Downtown," as well as the time of year it was, the clothes I wore, and my mom's mood. I was in the front seat of the car, my bare feet inches from touching the floorboard as Petula Clark belted out the words to "Downtown" over Mom's car radio. Mom effortlessly glided her giant Bat Mobile of a Cadillac up and down the curving country roads. Around each bend and turn, I remembered my childhood body having no power over the laws of gravity as each twist in the snakelike road before me caused my body to float along the slick leather seats. I thought to myself, "I can't wait to be old enough for my feet to touch the floorboard."

I called to mind my mom sharing her Coca-Cola with me. Back in those days, she put a small pack of salted nuts in her bottled Coke, long before sodas were sold in aluminum cans. I felt the cool soda pop bottle on my lips and experienced, for the first time, the soda's sweet carbonated tickle commingled with the zest of salty peanuts.

Mom smiled when I made a contorted face as the taste sensations swirled around in my mouth, burning my nose and causing my eyes to water. It was one of those rare warm and fuzzy episodes in my youth when everything felt just perfect, and I am almost positive it wasn't the gas bubbles in my stomach that caused my euphoria.

In one hundredth of a second, a distant memory flooded my consciousness, superimposing itself over my current reality more than 30 years later. During this multidimensional experience, it was effortless to feel both realities overlapping each other, creating a dual experience. It was a wonderful experience that pleasantly reminded me of the power of our subconscious mind.

The synchronicity of one song managed to erase space and time, 2,600 miles, and 32 years to be exact. The same song I heard when I was ten years old reactivated the same high feelings inside me in the fall of 2002, causing two worlds to unite in a climax of emotion and memory.

In the passenger's side of Max's car, I appreciated the healing quality of music and how it affects and changes our lives. As we sailed through the ravines of Laurel Canyon Boulevard, singing the words to "Downtown," I felt like a kid again, with that same funny taste in my memory, feeling pleased that my big toes almost touched the floorboard of that old Bat Mobile.

Music has that ability. It activates and awakens emotions within us. When we hear a song for the first time that makes us feel good, chances are that if we don't hear that same song for another 32 years, we will still feel good when we hear it again, and we will awaken and remember what we were doing, thinking, and feeling the first time we heard it.

Thought and feeling create more of our experience than all action and words put together. Whether the music we're enjoying is with or without lyrics, it is always the vibration of the music and the intention behind it that raises our individual frequency from common to extraordinary.

Can you recall the Coca-Cola commercial from the 70s, "I'd like to teach the world to sing in perfect harmony; I'd like to buy the world a Coke…"? I loved that ad campaign. I adored the way it felt and was captivated by its simple visual and auditory message. People of all races, colors, and creeds stood side by side in unison, singing and deliberately vibrating the verbal and "invisible fre- quency" of peace and harmony among all peoples.

The exact moments I experienced that Coke commercial, I believed it was possible to create harmony on a global level. The music appro- priated for a simple soft drink commercial actually brought desire and a pure belief for 30 seconds to the mass consciousness, causing us to hold the vision that all people can get along, if only for a few moments.

Music is a feeling medium that awakens our emotional attributes. These emotional attributes are extensions of our nonphysical energy, our Soul, if you will. As we marry the emotional aspects of our being to the physical aspects of our being, we can live a fulfilled experi- ence. Music offers an escape from our limited habit of thinking and feeling and gives us permission to forget the worry, fear, and con- cerns so we can live a better quality of life.

Listen to music that lifts your heart and soul. Sing all your favorite songs that carry you to the high points of your past and to the unlim- ited potential of your future. Choose a new theme song for yourself every week or so, and use each new theme song as your cheerleader, reminding you to think outside your normal, everyday reality. Allow the spirit of the music to awaken your soulful attributes and fuel your nonphysical desires into amazing physical manifestations.

One afternoon while reviewing some material, I had the TV on for background noise and was only half listening to VH-1. Suddenly, I heard the words to "It's the Real Thing" pouring out of the television set. Racing into the living room I saw my favorite commercial for Coca-Cola from the 70s displayed on the set with a commentary. It turns out my favorite commercial "musically speaking" is also the nation's favorite commercial as well. It was voted the number-one commercial of all time by VH-1.

BUT Blaster Six   **Praying with a Pure Heart**

"If the only prayer you say in your whole life is "Thank you," that would suffice."

—Meister Eckhart

Praying with a pure heart is simply praying with a rich emotional energy that feels like the outcome for which you are praying. If you are praying for happiness for yourself or for a loved one, you want to pray beyond physical words and action. You want to pray with the highest emotional frequency the cells and atoms in your physical body can muster.

Charles Haddon Spurgeon said, "Whether we like it or not, asking is the rule of the Kingdom." The purest form of asking is through prayer and authentic appreciation. Keep in mind that you are one with God Universe, that you are more nonphysical in your adult body than you are physical. We are born with the wisdom, knowledge, power, and love of the cosmos inside us. Our soul-self is infinite wisdom bringing our spiritual and human attributes together as one in order to fulfill our emotional frequencies.

The most powerful prayers we send are the ones launched from a platform of feeling excited, happy, uplifted and connected to our whole soul-self. The higher we raise our invisible frequencies inside our physical bodies, the faster our prayers are answered.

Another secret of praying purely is to talk about, observe, and vibrate the solution, or *SOUL*-ution, of our desires. We may want to change our old prayer habits to include lighthearted tools that speak to our unique belief systems.

As a child, I was raised to pray from a serious adult perspective. This approach took a lot of the animated electricity and plain ole fun out of praying.

In today's world, there are myriad ways to express our energy through the art of praying. We sing our prayers. We light candles and listen to music that matches the spirit of our prayers. We walk out in nature and appreciate the world around us. We follow alternative avenues of healing and new thought processes that revolutionize the old way of doing things, bringing these new perceptions into our old method of prayer.

Because I believe God has a great sense of humor, I firmly believe laughter, humor, and living life with a light heart and a fun-loving soul is a must-do action that facilitates our prayers being answered in record speed.

Music, prayer, chanting, affirmations, and just plain feeling good are powerful healing modalities. When we merge these powers together as ONE, every cell, atom, and molecule in our bodies resonates with its pure frequency.

Praying and chanting with music as a catalyst is an absolute Energetic Multiple Orgasmic Combustion Point®. Karen Drucker's music has masterfully perfected this art form. Her *Songs of the Spirit*

I, Songs of the Spirit II, and *Beloved* albums illustrate this example perfectly.

Karen's music is a permanent fixture in my home and heart. Her music is a series of brilliant vocals, chants, and song-ffirmations that marry our loving spirit and human selves together as one.

BUT Blaster Seven   Intuitive Intellect

"We should take care not to make the intellect our God; it has, of course, powerful muscles, but no personality."

—*Albert Einstein*

What is Intuitive Intellect? It is the moment the dreams we have dreamt since we were knee-high to a grasshopper come to us, circle us, and kiss us on the heart. It is when we know we are seen, heard, and felt by God Universe.

We have all had at least one experience in our lives when everything lined up, and we felt on our game. Our heart was full, our mind clear, and our spiritual self-esteem at a heavenly high.

Intuitive Intellect is a light that shines from inside our heart, mind, and feelings out to the world. Hollywood calls this quality the infamous "It" faculty. You've heard the term, "She's the new *It Girl?*" As a teenager, back in my day, a big *It Girl* in the music industry was Donna Summer, the queen of disco. In my twenties, it was Madonna, and the last few years it has been Britney Spears. We all know what happens when three pop diva, *It Girls* get together to perform the opening act of the MTV Music Awards? Yeah, the kiss that was heard around the world. "It" was something else, wasn't it?

The bare bones of owning Intuitive Intellectual magic are:

A. To believe in our dreams with BUT-Free abandon and

B. To think thoughts with instinct, emotional power, and self-esteem that possess pure love and liquid logic.

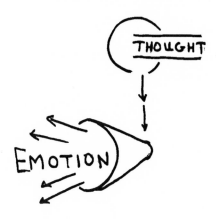

I believe all things come from nonphysical consciousness first and into physical reality second. Once we're born into human bodies, we are still infinitely connected to our nonphysical consciousness.

The beauty of being human is our free will to eternally choose what we want to choose. It has been my experience that when we choose hi-frequency patterns of thought, we garner extraordinary, and often miraculous, results. When we choose to channel our attention into lo-frequency formats, we garner negative, or at best, ordinary, results.

Every Friday without fail, I meet my friend Victor Benoun for our instinctual brainstorming meeting in Studio City. Together, we day-dream and amplify business concepts and ideas. We have a blast supporting each other in our goals and future aspirations. As a matter of fact, it was Victor's idea that I take the simple BIG BUT class outline I was teaching and turn it into this book format. A little over one year later, after lots of hikes and meetings with my dream team, this little bitty BUT Book is done. Many great ideas come from our lunch meetings together. Victor's next books, *Your Lemonade Stand On the Corner* and *Everything I Know I Learned Walking My Dog,* are currently in the works as I write this entry.

I use Victor as an example of Intuitive Intellect because we each believe in our dreams with BUT-Free abandon. We use our instinct, emotional power, and self-esteem with love and a genuine passion for what we do for a living.

BUT FACT:

When you believe in your dreams purely, you will attract new people into your life who radiate pure, supportive energy toward making your dreams a reality.

From birth, we are trained to observe (OVAL Mirror) the physical world through the lens of our intellectual properties first. This is a left-brain function. As physical reality-based entities, we are trained and conditioned to choose our physically-focused perspective over our right-brain focus, our feelings, and our heart.

When we observe the world through our intellectual eyes, without appreciation for our heart, feelings, or creativity, we are literally slamming the door on our Soul Attributes.

Imagine having unlimited power to create amazing good for yourself and others, and having a direct laser line to the Universe with a Soul agreement stating the Universe will deliver whatever your heart desires. All you have to do is harmonize your thoughts, feelings, and heart as ONE, and the manifestation soon follows. Can you imagine how different our lives would be with direct conscious contact with the Universe? Our Intuitive Intellect is our laser-linked Soul communication with our Universal Mind.

Imagine a golden-white light directed from the heart of the Universe to us. It is an actual holographic beam emanating an all-knowing, healing vibration reminding us of our true origin. This ribbon of focused light originates in the Universe, superimposing itself in a figure-eight symbol through our bodies. This vibratory figure-eight symbol integrates our brain, body, and spirit as ONE.

To function from our Intuitive Intellect is to consciously choose to observe life through our Soul's perspective first and through our human eyes second. This new habit eventually leads us to seeing the world through our human-soul potential.

Intuitive Intellect illustrates the power of perfect harmony and complimentary balance within our right and left brain, while shining a universal spotlight on the power of our heart and feelings. Each component mentioned—the right brain, heart, solar plexus, and left brain—is genuinely designed to share equal billing on this stage called Earth as we live in the spotlight of our Soul.

As Souls first, we are born with an innate connection to our soul's expression through our Intuitive Intellect®. We communicate with the Universe through our nonphysical strengths. Each thought we think activates a nonphysical frequency. Thoughts that feel good activate hi-frequencies while negative thoughts active lo-frequencies. The more pure and creative our intuitive *right-brain* thoughts are while in harmony with our left hemisphere, the more successful our lives become.

Imagine a simple figure eight situated inside your body. Imagine the "8" begins in your right brain. The "8" moves gracefully through your heart center, continuing around your Solar Plexus Megaphone®, looping back up through and intersecting your heart center a second time, then curves around into your left brain. Once the "8" is complete, it reconnects to your right brain and continues the figure-eight pattern, repeating infinitely.

The objective for radiating our figure eight or Intuitive Intellect symbol in the order mentioned is to continue to heighten our invisible frequencies in harmony with our physical realities. The faster our figure eight vibrates on all four cylinders, the faster we are in accordance with creating our personal heaven on Earth.

The longer we feel positive frequencies, the more abundant and steady our Intuitive Intellect resonates. Then, it perpetuates a creative mind, open heart, and healthy self-esteem, guiding our heart in a brilliant correspondence with our logic thinking brain.

Abraham-Hicks says that absolute genius is paying attention to one subject purely. We're all created equal from our soul's perspective. All people are born with healthy intuition as well as the tools to pretend, fantasize, daydream, and make believe our own individual magic.

The Vital Components

The fabulous four components used to activate, vibrate, and perpetuate our Intuitive Intellectual wisdom are, in this order:

1-Right Brain

2-Heart Chakra

3-Solar Plexus

4-Heart Chakra

5-Left Brain

1-Right Brain	2/4 Heart Chakra	3-Solar Plexus	5-Left Brain
Art Awareness	Emotional Power	Personal Power	Reasoning Skills
Imagination	Oneness with Life	Self-esteem	Written Language
Ideas & Instinct	Love & Affinity	Forming of Self	Science Skills
Music Awareness	Compassion	Authority	Number Skills
Left-hand Control	Nuturing	Self-confidence	Right-hand Control

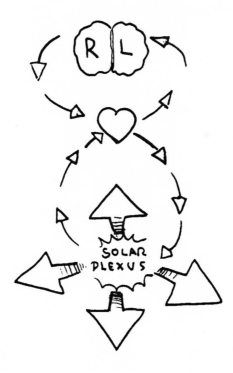

A more detailed description of each area the figure eight ties together is as follows.

Our Right Brain endows us with the infinite treasures of imagination, ideas, intuition, instinct, art awareness, three-dimensional forms, musical awareness, connection to the subconscious, and our left-hand control.

Our Heart Chakra reminds us we come from an invisible sea of unconditional love. The heart and soul of God Universe is unconditional love.

Chakras are invisible energy centers consistently radiating our soul truth, despite the fact that we habitually focus on the negative (lo-frequency vocabulary and feelings).

As stated above, the heart chakra is unconditional love personified. Our Universal Heart has never focused on prejudice, judgment, hurt, or negative emotion. The heart chakra is eternally locked onto the vibration and realization of beauty, essence of spirit, unconditional acceptance, and allowing one's soul to express love through our physical form.

The heart chakra is unique because it is neither of the Earth nor of Heaven. Rather, it is a grounding point between the two. Our heart chakra brings our Heaven aspects into a harmonic concordance with our Earth aspects so we can live the life we were meant to live.

I was taught that when our heart chakra reviews our history of love relationships, it only recalls and remembers the good, hi-frequency experiences. It retraces the beauty, love, and all the good experiences we've lived through. Today, in our present moment experience, it sees the same thing. When the heart chakra looks into our future, it knows and believes our prince or princess charming is there, that our life can be full, happy, and overflowing with true love.

All we have to do is get the heck out of our own way. The best way to allow our heart to work on our behalf is stop with the BIG BUTS.

If we put a personality type with our heart chakra it would be optimistic, happy, appreciative, pure of spirit, and would view the glass as half full. Each moment we feel inspired, passionate, giddy, sensual, attractive, electric, or good, our heart is whispering to our mind, body, and soul.

Next, our God Ribbon "8" circles and cradles our solar plexus. The solar plexus is housed just above the stomach. It governs the positive aspects of our self-esteem, self-confidence, self-worth, and freedom of choice.

I've understood the solar plexus chakra to be used to interpret our vibratory feelings based on our thoughts. For example, when we think a thought, we vibrate a frequency in the solar plexus about that thought. Our mind and solar plexus are invisibly joined at the hip. When we observe something with our eyes open, we will think and vibrate. The same is true when we observe things in our imagination; we will invariably think and vibrate. When most people think about money, they usually vibrate a lo-frequency about it.

Many of us work hard to generate enough money to live paycheck to paycheck. The real question is, what thoughts are we thinking while working hard to make enough money to survive? If we're thinking lo-frequency thoughts, we're also vibrating lo-frequency signals.

A lo-frequency signal is the equivalent of a poverty vibration. A poverty vibration in our solar plexus brings us more poverty in our reality. In this example, we've unconsciously created more lack of money, which really means a lack of freedom for most of us.

Since this is how I personally perceive the solar plexus chakra, I've added a fun twist to playfully remind myself that every second, I AM creating my life with invisible thought patterns that jumpstart invisible vibrations that bring me physical manifestations.

Da-da-da-dumm! Ladies and gentleman, please welcome to the podium, your Solar Plexus Spotlight.

As we think thoughts, we vibrate feelings in our solar plexus chakra. The solar plexus then spotlights this feeling and projects its frequency into the heart and soul of the Universe. The Universe then delivers back to us more of what we have been vibrating. Then we live the experience we vibrated (The Oval Mirror).

After circling the solar plexus, the figure "8" threads itself back through the heart center a second time, anchoring new high-vibratory thought and feeling patterns with pure love on its way to our logical left brain.

Our left brain governs our reasoning, logical thinking, scientific skills, written language, number skills, spoken language, and our right-hand control.

Our Heaven Chakras

include the

Crown Center, Third Eye and Throat

Our Heart Chakra is

suspended between

Heaven and Earth

Our Earth Chakras

include the

Root, Sacral and Solar Plexus

Since childhood, I have sensed that each moment we feel hi-frequency goodness, our Earth Self and Heaven Self converge in a dance of oneness causing our heart to overflow with pure, unconditional, invisible emotion. This is the epitome of operating in life from the Intuitive Intellect and it is the best time to follow our inner instinct and inner voice.

In these moments, our tiny physical bodies often cannot contain the huge level of invisible Universal Energy that is pouring through us. Examples of physical reactions to the invisible influence of our Intuitive Intellect are:

Angel bumps or flesh bumps

Hair standing on our heads and arms

Teary eyes

Psychic hits

That warm fuzzy *déjà vu* experience

Electromagnetic impulses vibrating through us

Absolute knowing

Gut instinct and

The famed Hallelujah Moment.

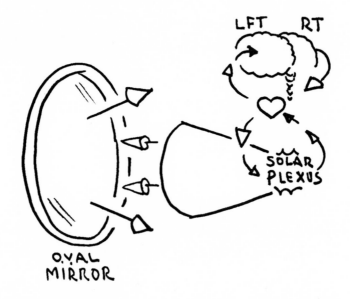

Fortunately, these side effects don't hit us simultaneously. Can you imagine what that would look like? Or better yet, how it would feel to experience all of them at the same time?

We are born with Intuitive Intellect activated within us. This way of thinking and being is innate, normal. Intuition in and of itself is a direct connection to the nonphysical world and to our Soul Electricity. Most psychics will tell you that receiving psychic impressions feels like their imagination, not their logical mind.

Babies are born with the leverage of the Universe behind them, supporting and guiding them. Everyone on the planet is intuitive, heartfelt art in action that is fueled by God's ingrained self-esteem and self-worth.

Hold on to your dreams. Don't let them die without pursuing them. Breathe life into them and give them permission to come to you full of surprises beyond belief.

Living Outside the TRY-Angle

> *"Many things—such as loving, going to sleep, or behaving unaffectedly—are done worst when we try hardest to do them."*
>
> —*Clive Staples Lewis*

I love studying thought patterns and belief systems in consciousness. I find it one of the more fascinating and rewarding things to observe. Through my studies, I have learned to identify a concept I have coined as the TRY-Angle Personality®. When our TRY-Angle personality appears, it means we have slammed the door on our Intuitive Intellectual properties, stripping ourselves of the Universe's unlimited power.

We've all heard the old adage, "If at first you don't succeed, try, try again." That seems to sum up many of our lives.

How often do we *Try* really hard to make it, *Try* to get by? Or, *Try* to hang on just a little bit longer? How about when we feel low and someone says we should *Try* to think positive and "if we're lucky" a light will eventually shine upon us rewarding us for our struggles.

Try means to test in order to determine effect, worth, or desirability. Try is to make an effort, to subject to great strain or hardship. Angle is to *try* to get something by using schemes, tricks, or other artful means.

TRY-Angle®: To effort, strain, or scheme while using cunning means in order to attain what we believe we are worthy of or deserve to have in life.

The TRY-Angle describes one of our greatest physical plights. Because we have a habit of forgetting our Soul Electricity (our eternal higher selves) and replacing it with what we see, hear, touch, taste, and smell, we habitually trap ourselves in a vicious cycle of TRYING. Trying too hard to do any task locks us into the density of our three-dimensional personality and slams the door on our multidimensional power.

TRY-Angles are often kindhearted and spiritual in nature, and have been known on more than one occasion to give others the shirt off their own backs. My friend Jill Lloyd and I were talking one afternoon about metaphysics. Jill used the term "cautiously optimistic" to describe her desire to move forward with an important project in her life. Despite feeling gun-shy about past experiences, she was moving forward with her endeavor. I fell in love with her perspective and fun choice of words and realized many people felt the way she did. I know there were many times in my past when I was *cautiously optimistic* about the big three: love, money, and career.

For the most part, TRY-Angle people honestly believe what they were taught as children and work exceptionally hard to live by the rules set for them by other TRY-Angle personalities from their past.

The greatest misfortune of being a TRY-Angle is their dreaming slowly stops and the desire soon dies because it hurts them to desire something they believe they may never attain. TRY-Angle persons often observe the physical world around them, forgetting they have the power of the Universe behind them, supporting and speaking to them through the power of their heart, feelings, and imagination.

TRY-Angle personalities are classic doers, movers, and shakers. They seem to get nervous at the thought of grass growing under their feet. They are usually uncomfortable asking for help and would rather do everything themselves, because TRY-Angle people believe no one else can do it right or as well as they can. As one TRY-Angle person said to me, "It's just easier to do it myself than to go back later and correct what someone else has done wrong."

TRY-Angle people overextend, overachieve, and are multitasking individuals. This vibratory behavior eventually leads to their feeling burned out, not appreciated, and/or underpaid.

Their internal dialogue can sound a little bit like this: "I do my best to help everyone else, and I don't understand why no one helps me when I need it." Or: "I work my BUT off and I have so little to show for it." Basically, the emotional message from the TRY-Angle personality to the world and Universe is, *"Life isn't fair."*

BUT FACT:

Using the word BUT isn't bad. It is our dramatic contradiction in emotions when we use the word BUT that is ultimately bad for us.

Having been a TRY-Angle person for years (why do you think I wrote this book?), I finally realized this attitude was a recipe for failure and defeat—neither of which TRY-Angles will easily admit to themselves or anyone else, unless their exhaustion finally lands them in the emergency room after passing out at a supermarket grand-opening with thousands of onlookers, while purchasing cookies and *Pepto-Bismol*. This is the moment I knew I had to take a day off…duh!

I had set myself up and created a world around me in which I did not feel supported, seen, or heard. I believed if anything was going to get done right at a grueling, breakneck pace, I would have to do it myself. And I was right—not because I actually lacked the support from friends or family, BUT because my BUT Belief was that I was not supported. As a result, everywhere I looked and everything I did proved me right. TRY-Angles are usually right to a fault. I had strong willpower, and I worked two and often three jobs at a time. I was taught that working hard and being a good person would get me the nice things in life, things I deserved and things I worked extra hard to earn and be worthy of. BUT I felt exhausted, tired, and invisible to the powers that be. Now that was a lo-frequency place to be in. It is no wonder I woke up the second time in the back of an ambulance, immediately worrying how much it would cost for the one-mile ride from the supermarket to the hospital with the bells and whistles.

Let's revisit the TRY-Angle pattern: Working hard, doing too much, and multitasking with great effort. Wanting help BUT not asking for help. Having a desire for input and validation BUT unconsciously pushing it all away with my nonphysical vibratory belief of, I have to do everything myself. My action and work ethics have always been there. They still are, AND today, the hard work is coupled with doing what I love AND with being of service by sharing information I feel will uplift AND empower others everywhere.

Today, I choose to see myself in a new light and open myself to the aspects of my soul's electricity and sharing my passion. It has been with this feel-good attitude that I've stepped out of the TRY-Angle. It is my desire that you will, too.

How many of us have fallen in the quicksand of this pattern at some point in life? Sometimes, we are in this vicious cycle for a small amount of time, while there are other periods when we cannot seem to escape the negative and worrisome spiral of plummeting finances, hurtful love affairs, or our bad jobs for months and years on end.

This is a normal, "perceived reality" among hardworking, good-hearted persons. The TRY-Angle enters the picture because there seems to be a perpetual try-hard, struggle-hard, effort-hard formula TRY-Angle Personalities are literally dying to be free of.

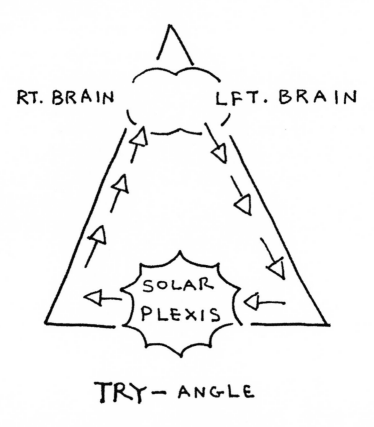

This pattern begins with the first of three angles, which I believe more than 90% of the people in the United States move through:

1.   First it's the Left Brain: The left hemisphere of our brain is the compartment of logic, physical action, and words. Most people bang their way through life working hard and getting back little or nothing. Hard work and lots of action with little or no vibration to run off of makes life a struggle. Focusing on the physical reality without the use of emotions, a full heart, or a creative thought makes our life lifeless.

2.   Next is step two of the TRY-Angle personality, or Feelings: TRY-Angle personalities are often null, numb, or void after awhile. Feelings are second in their plan to create the life they want. Feelings are on the back burner behind the habitually engrained hard-work attitude. More often than not, throughout history and today, our feelings are not considered a strong "realistic attribute" in the art of creating the life we want.

3.   Lastly comes our amazing umbilical cord to All That Is, our Right Brain: Creativity, intuition, imagination, and pretending are often thrown out with the bath water. The only imagining our TRY-Angle personality affords us is worry, fear, anxiety, unfairness, and, dare I say, victim mentality. Because so many TRY-Angles have spent endless years working their BUTS off in the real world, they have been taught to believe their creative, artistic, and intuitive attributes are worthless in life. Not to mention they are told their right brain, heart attributes, or hi-frequency emotions do not get the mortgage paid. In other words, "You have to be realistic and responsible and get a real job that has benefits." Over the years, TRY-Angles wait for their hard work to pay off before they allow themselves the luxury of enjoying their hearts' desires and allowing their dreams to come true. A great illustration of this step is when TRY-Angles say things like: "I'll take art classes after I pay off my debt" or "I'll take my vacation after I get everything else done first."

Recapping the TRY-Angle personality to understand their pattern of living life is to first see them focus on the logical, real world; to work hard based on their logical reasoning, to do what they are taught, and to do it without asking if there is another way to have their experience be or feel happier.

They lock themselves away from their true power and essence. Their feelings are seen as not important and unrealistic. Numbing their feelings, they drudge forward in love, money, and career, working themselves into early graves because their spirit cannot contact them through their very emotions.

And lastly, the imagination their right brain delivers is predominately based on their left-brain thinking. This lo-frequency pattern of thinking and living activates the Biggest Ass BUTS of all.

This is the key faculty to thought patterns like, "I really do want to fall in love, BUT I'm afraid the jerk will hurt me again." In examples like this, TRY-Angle people's ability to think or see beyond their past experiences holds them enslaved to their Past-Tense Selves. Their desires are high enough; however, their BUT Beliefs trump their heartfelt emotion with old programming based on their history.

They have a desire to break free from these outdated beliefs, BUT their imagination is used to scare them into playing it safe, keeping it real. Their life grows more complicated as their feelings and instincts are buried deep inside the wells of the reality they can see, touch, taste, hear, and smell.

BUT Blaster Eight   **Vibratory Vocabulary**

"One forgets words and one forgets names. One's vocabulary needs constant fertilization or it will die."

—*Evelyn Waugh*

Every word in every language radiates an invisible vibratory frequency. Even our names and birthdates, when spoken aloud, register energetic vibration. For example, many psychics will often ask you to write or speak your full birth name or date of birth in order to receive an electromagnetic impulse. It is the invisible vibration of our vocabulary that carries energy inside it. Healers and energy interpreters can sense, feel, and know things based on these vibrations.

Everyone knows what vocabulary is, BUT few people realize the words they are using could be the very thing that stops their desired good from coming to them. For example, how many times have you used the word "money" in your thoughts and words?

More often than not, the word "money" has a low, lethargic vibration that surrounds it. It is not using the word that brings us the money, it is how we ultimately feel about the green stuff that determines whether we can consistently magnetize it to us or not.

Bernice Kanner, author of *Are You Normal About Money,* says "One in five Americans confessed that they often worry about money. Fifty-five percent think about it only when they're managing it, and 23 percent let their minds drift to it occasionally."

How do you FEEL when you think about the subject of money? Can you feel prosperous while observing it in your mind's eye?

Or a better question is, when you get your paycheck at the end of a long, hard work week, do you feel it is a fair exchange of money to compensate you for all your hard work? Or do you feel it is not an appropriate match to the number of hours you've put in?

If you answered that you don't feel the monetary compensation is fair for the number of hours you worked, you are vibrating a lo-frequency about the word money. Or, better stated: If you are saying affirmations to attract more money to yourself, there is a great chance you are radiating a lo-frequency vibration each and every time you think the word money, say the word money, and take action toward making more money. This is the ultimate BIG BUT in that you are saying and doing all of the right things, BUT you are vibrating a lo-frequency vibration that is literally keeping your money at bay, regardless of how hard you work to obtain more of the green stuff.

Each of us desires money for different reasons. I would say the primary reason for wanting more money is because we believe it will bring us one or more of the following:

Comfort	Security	Flexibility	Assurance
Freedom	Ease	Release	Sanctuary
Spontaneity	Independence	Relief	Solace

In the space below, write the word "money" five times in a row.

Does the feeling of this word vibrate a high, pure frequency? Or, does it vibrate a low, heavy frequency? If you felt a heaviness in your Solar Plexus Megaphone®, you are asking for the money you want and feeling the lack of money at the same time.

Now, pick one of the words listed below that you feel has a high, pure frequency. Write it five times slowly, paying attention to how it vibrates in your body while writing it.

Comfort	Security	Flexibility	Assurance
Freedom	Ease	Release	Sanctuary
Spontaneity	Independence	Relief	Solace

Again, does the feeling of your new vibratory vocabulary feel like a high, pure frequency, or a low, heavy frequency?

Make a conscious choice to use all the vocabulary you can that radiates a high vibration. The higher the vibration, the faster your desires come to you. The sooner you use the art of vibratory vocabulary, the sooner you eliminate the BIG BUT Syndrome from your life. Happy vibrating!

BUT Blaster Nine   Energetic Multiple Orgasmic Combustion Points®

"You see me in my most virile moment when you see me doing what I do. When I am directing, a special energy comes upon me…It is only when I am doing my work that I feel truly alive. It is like having sex.

—*Federico Fellini*

Have you had your Energetic Multiple Orgasmic Combustion Point today? If not, you don't know what you're missing! What is an Energetic Multiple Orgasmic Combustion Point?

In a nutshell, it is what Oprah calls a "Hallelujah Moment." A great example of an EMOCP in action was when Cuba Gooding Jr. won his first Oscar for the movie *Jerry McGuire*. He was ecstatic, beaming, and through the roof, to the point he could no longer contain his electricity. He began shouting bounds of appreciation as he leapt and danced near his microphone.

The longer Cuba expressed his heartfelt gratitude through joyous eyes and his notorious smile, the more people in the Academy Awards audience felt compelled to leap to their feet. The audience began reflecting Cuba's electricity back to him, thus creating an extraordinary exchange of soulful energy. It was no surprise he received a bit of a standing ovation in absolute appreciation.

The American Heritage Dictionary defines the following words as:

Energetic: possessing, displaying or exerting energy.

Multiple: having or consisting of more than one individual, element, part, or other component.

Orgasmic: Any intense excitement.

Combustible: Easily aroused or excited.

Point: any distinct condition or degree: *The point of no return*

Energetic Multiple Orgasmic Combustion Point: Possessing and sustaining a hi-frequency energy while multiplying that excitement numerous times until one achieves a layered combustible emotion.

I enjoy taking mundane, daily life experiences and adding a series of Energetic Multiple Orgasmic Combustion Points (or EMOCP) to them in order to eliminate the BIG BUT Syndrome®. Doing this gives me continued opportunities to expand the way I think about, feel, and perceive my life. Charles Dickens said, "Reflect upon your present blessings, of which every man has many…not on your past misfortunes, of which all men have some."

A good example is what I refer to as the **Past Tense Me** verses the **Present Moment Me**. Like so many other patrons around me, the **Past Tense Me** stood in line at a local retail establishment, getting more irritated and impatient about the lack of good customer service.

I tapped my foot, checked my watch, and sheepishly studied the slow clerk behind the counter, getting more frustrated as the second hand on my watch ticked away the remainder of my day.

The more judgmental I was, the more anxious I became. The more anxious I became, the more I sent out lo-frequency signals, ultimately creating the physical stagnation of the line in which I stood.

Looking through the lens of the **Past Tense Me**, I remember standing in these establishments thinking, "If I were the cashier, I would be more professional." Or, "They should call someone from the back for assistance and communicate with their customers better."

I looked at my watch again. The person in front of me sighed, checked her watch, and counted the number of customers in the line ahead of us.

Two people behind me discussed the horrible service loud enough for the single clerk to hear them. "It's like this every time I come in here!" the elderly man behind me exclaimed, glancing around to be sure everyone heard him. The young lady next to him readjusted her once sleeping baby and the three packages she was juggling. "I know," she affirmed, "I would leave, but I've already waited ten minutes, and I'll have to wait in line somewhere else if I leave now."

In my **Past Tense Me** life, this was a common phenomenon riddling my daily experience, making me responsible for consistently being at the wrong place at the wrong time. Whether it was bumper-to-bumper traffic, a rude clerk at the bank, or attracting another jerk, I slowly noticed a pattern of negative things happening to me, and I wanted to know why.

I began to realize the more I observed negative people, places, and things around me that I attracted more negativity. The more I chose to observe pleasant, "hi-frequency" people, places, and things, I attracted more pleasant outcomes.

Today, when I am standing in line, I utilize the power of my **Present Moment ME** with **EMOCP** to consciously create consistent hi-frequency circumstances.

Before walking into an establishment, **Present Moment Me** thinks "hi-frequency" thoughts. I focus on thoughts that activate good feelings, and I begin to multiply the thoughts from there. For instance, I may choose a song that makes me feel good and run it in my mind. I often use memories or a series of thoughts that make me smile. Doing this in my Present Moment experience amplifies my nonphysical attributes in a hi-frequency output. In other words, I radiate a pure energetic combustion point.

Once I reach my destination, in this case the post office, I pay attention to the elements I appreciate (this is a great opportunity to use the **TAGS Technique**). I first observe the establishment itself—its fixtures, signage, windows, and such. Next, I focus on the patrons—what they're wearing, their physical attributes, and the way they interact with others.

While standing in line, **Present Moment Me** scans all the aspects of the environment that feel good, then I compound those aspects with other orgasmic elements.

The **Present Moment Me** makes a deliberate choice to look at all aspects that radiate high frequencies. I can appreciate the innocence of the sleeping baby and its mother for being considerate enough to fill out her forms for the clerk before she gets in line. The thoughtful gentleman who opened the door for the elderly man reminds me that kindness still makes my heart sing.

I read the store signage that applies to my transaction and am grateful for its detailed information and appreciate the time and effort it took an employee to hang this sign nice and straight so it is effortless to read.

I observe each generous and polite gesture the clerks use while interacting with the patrons. I am thankful each time I see, hear, and feel the clerk say, "Next in line please." I am grateful someone from the back of the post office came to the front counter to ask if anyone had a pick-up with no money exchanged, because the couple in front of me said "yes," and now I am at the front of the line, and the clerk calls me.

The second scenario applies to mild usage of Energetic Multiple Orgasmic Combustion Points while doing mundane errands. The only purpose for this is to expand your thoughts and feelings to higher frequencies. The higher the frequency, the greater the physical results you will create.

This afternoon, my friend Jeff Mayse called moments before I wrote this chapter. Jeff is an accomplished actor and writer. The two of us discussed the different techniques we use to inspire and promote continued enthusiasm while writing. Both of us do our best to choose hi-frequency environments that promote our creative-artistic energy in order to create our desired outcome.

Jeff goes "on location" to write his stories and scripts longhand, often choosing a physical environment that matches the frequency of his writing project. It is not unusual for Jeff to drive an hour and a half to places like Disneyland or some hole-in-the-wall coffee shop in an odd corner of town to achieve oneness with the energy of his project.

I, on the other hand, had trouble writing for years. The **Past Tense Me** received well-earned C's and D's in English. Back then, I just couldn't get the hang of the whole left-brain writing thing. Any time I had a deadline for an important project, I would shut down and put so much pressure (lo-frequency feelings) on myself that I couldn't seem to buck my own current belief about "not being enough."

I realized during my conversation with Jeff that over the years, I have taken his idea and streamlined it to custom-fit my new current beliefs about writing. Today, when I sit down to write, I leave the **Past Tense Me** outside my office, because the **Past Tense Me** has lo-frequency beliefs about "not being good enough." This outdated aspect of me remembers the mediocre grade-point average I received in school and doesn't want to relive the negative emotion from the past.

Now, I actively promote the **Present Moment Me** with a full bag of **EMOCP** tricks, bridging my old beliefs with my new desire. This ultimately eliminates my former BIG BUT beliefs with newly elevated emotions. How?

Before I go to my office, I establish the first series of hi-frequency feelings. This causes me to radiate high energy before I write the first word. Once I'm in the office, I begin to overlap and multiply the combustion points.

My office is comfortable; it is a good place to accomplish my creative projects. The walls surround me with beautiful paintings from my tours to Peru, China, and North America. I have research materials at my immediate disposal. The lighting is perfect for my taste. I can see outside to a beautiful couple of acres of manicured landscaping, and beyond a gorgeous mountain that towers above.

While writing, I turn on my ceiling fan, light candles, and play music to match the mood of what I am creating. I place strategic items around me that enhance my desire, promote the end result, and empower me to continue the momentum I have started.

Each one of the things I mentioned evokes feelings from me in and of itself, however, I multiply the energy of each one to generate "feel-good excitement." This creates a series of energetic combustion points multiplied to enrich my intention to write.

In short, surround yourself with as many fun and uplifting things as you can find to activate an environment for yourself. The longer you can sustain a hi-frequency feeling while working on a project, the better your physical results will be.

How can you multiply the Energetic Multiple Orgasmic Combustion Points in the areas of your life in order to get more energetic bang for your vibratory buck?

BUT Blaster Ten   Artistic Creative Expression

"Each of us makes his own weather, determines the color of the skies in the emotional universe which he inhabits."

—*Fulton J. Sheen*

I have heard it said that God Universe is the ultimate artist, the greatest creator, and each of us is a co-creator with God. I believe this. Artistic creativity originates in the nonphysical world. This creative force then races toward the Earth plane, pouring to and through anyone who is an open channel to receive its unconditional gifts.

We ourselves are actual God Art originating in the nonphysical realm. With a combination of our freewill to choose and our parents' intention to give birth to us, we moved our unlimited consciousness to Earth, where we blended our Universal Self into a physical personality.

From our nonphysical point of view, we clearly understand that our essential energy creates our physical experience. Our soul instincts remind us that our every thought and feeling entertains and influences the world around us. The same thoughts and feelings that designed and sculpted our invisible realities then are, in this exact moment, sculpting our life today.

Feeling creative or expressing art from a creative platform generates an amazing vortex of timeless energy that encompasses our physical personality. In comparison, our human shell is merely a grain of sand in the grand scheme, and our soul is actually God Universe. In essence, our body and soul are one and the same, not separate. This means we have unlimited co-creative power to sculpt both our physical reality and nonphysical reality alike.

We are a masterpiece imagined from the heart and soul of the ultimate artist, God Universe. Just as Michelangelo created the sculpture David or Leonardo Da Vinci painted the Mona Lisa, God Universe created the ultimate living art, us! It is my strong belief that over time, the art and artist are designed and created to become one.

Recently, I met RJ Durell and Nick Florez, both professional dancers and both artists who used their Soul Electricity to paint on the physical canvas of their lives. RJ and Nick have danced with icons in the music and movie industry. For most people, what would be a once-in-a-lifetime opportunity to meet their favorite stars is a lifestyle for RJ and Nick.

I asked RJ when he consciously knew in his heart he was destined to dance professionally. He replied that he had always known. He recalled knowing at the tender age of three that he wanted to dance. RJ booked his first audition off a dance scholarship he won as a teenager and shortly after, he was dancing on tour with Cher.

I also asked him how it felt to dance on stage in front of fifty thousand screaming fans. RJ recollected, "The moment I stepped from behind the curtain and onto the stage, the wind was knocked out of me. It was like an out-of-body experience."

Nick described how artists like Madonna, Janet Jackson, and others inspired him. As a child, Nick felt a strong connection to their music, dance, and creative expression. I asked Nick when he realized he wanted to be a professional dancer. "I gravitated to material like Janet Jackson's *Rhythm Nation* and Madonna's *Truth or Dare* movie." These documentaries, with their behind-the-scenes footage of the dancers, props, and artistic direction, grabbed Nick's imagination and burning desire. In these moments, Nick felt the world he observed and appreciated on the TV screen would someday be the world in which he would dance.

Nick has completed a tour with Britney Spears and is now touring with Janet Jackson. Today, Nick and RJ can be seen on the big and small screens living out their childhood dreams.

It is true everything around us is a genuinely felt, creative expression. Pure art is genius. John Hersey said, "True genius rearranges old material in a way never seen before." By definition, a person who performs his or her work as if it were art, is an artist.

From a mansion in the Hollywood Hills to a cardboard box housing the homeless, we design our reality with the power of free will, observation, and choice. When I was a kid, I overheard my mom tell my aunt, "Eddie is good at making chicken salad out of chicken sh—." I didn't know exactly what she meant at the time. I do know that it felt good to me when I heard it.

We all have the ability to take nothing and turn it into a masterpiece. Or better stated, even if we are living in a poverty environment, we absolutely have the ability to take our soul attributes of pretending, imagining, daydreaming, and fantasizing and turn how we perceive our poverty environment into something that feels and vibrates a feel-good, prosperity consciousness.

We have the free will to observe what we choose to observe. What we choose to observe causes us to feel either high or low pulsations of emotional energy. God Universe then responds to these pulsations by bringing us the physical manifestation caused by our invisible pulsations.

Every pulsation we emanate is a creation, an expression of our soul and human personality. Every pulsation we generate enhances either our prosperity or our poverty consciousness.

As an artist observing negativity, we will create more negativity on the canvas of our life. Likewise, a soul artist observing beauty creates a life filled with beautiful, artful experiences.

An artist who utilizes his or her soul electricity consistently in daily life would look something like this: You are an artist with unlimited potential. You love harnessing inspirational ideas and creative solutions. You are revered for donating your time, energy, and creativity to the masses while making the world a better place to live through your generous accomplishments. In a few short years you, your art, and your humanitarian contributions are synonymous with global achievement and genuine greatness.

Everything you touch turns to gold. You take complete responsibility for creating your life through your feelings and emotions. You are loved, and you have captured the richest meaning of self-love and self-esteem. You appreciate the extravagant lifestyle you have produced while doing what you enjoy. You have great friends, a lovely partner, a beautiful home, and financial freedom. You are living your purpose and fulfilling your destiny. You are on top of the world.

Meanwhile, a lo-frequency artist may look something like this: You are painting on the canvas of life with your mundane thoughts and numbed feelings. You dip your brush into the endless colors of thought available, and the instant your paintbrush touches your canvas, the brilliant paint colors immediately fade into lifeless, mustard yellow. Frustrated, you reach for a cold lump of clay to mold and sculpt it into a beautiful relationship. The clay is bulky, resistant, and doesn't do what you want it to do in order to make you happy. You blame the clay for not turning out the way you wanted it to. The clay fades to a mustard yellow hue of nothingness.

Desperate to express your creative essence, you decide on one last-ditch attempt to create happiness. Irritated, you decided you'll write poetry, music, or a bestselling book that uplifts people. The poetry is harder than you thought. The music feels good, BUT there are more starving musicians than rich ones. The book isn't writing itself as you'd planned. At this point, the poetry, music, and book also disappear into the same raggedy, everyday yellow that refuses to allow you the freedom of expressing your invisible desire on the physical canvas of life.

Finally, you give up. The authority figures were right. You can't get by in life just dreaming and imagining on the creative and artistic side of life. After all, it's not realistic, and it is certainly not making you a responsible, play-by-the-rules citizen. So, you give up and seek out that safe, dependable, 9-to-5 job and let go of your soul artistry.

We've all had the experience of taking the brilliant colors life offers and painting a reality with those colors only to see that our end result is bland yellow instead of the vibrant masterpiece we began. Art, like all things, takes practice, patience, and a playful approach. The first time our paintbrush touches the canvas, it usually doesn't represent what we see in our imagination. In fact, it often looks kind of scary.

We are here to explore the animation of our imagination, to perform new techniques in our thoughts and physically place both on this canvas called the human experience. Over time, with playful practice strokes, the colors of our imagination become fine-tuned, realistically aligned, and physically beautiful. Our pretend dreams become a physical reality, for what we imagine in our minds and feelings eventually becomes what we live and breathe.

This is life.

Which artist do you identify with most, the first artist on top of the world or the frustrated artist experiencing life through the complacent monotone lens?

As an artist who creates life, what is your free will, choice, and observation locked onto?

Are you observing the art of physical poverty or observing the art of pleasant prosperity?

BUT Blaster Eleven **Visualization and Imagination**

"Just because a man lacks the use of his eyes doesn't mean he lacks vision."

—*Stevie Wonder*

You cannot talk about the art of visualizing without thinking about Shakti Gawain and her monumental accomplishments with the books *Creative Visualization* and *The Creative Visualization Workbook—Use the Power of Your Imagination to Create What You Want in Your Life.* I have always believed imagination and focused feelings create our lives. Shakti set a superb standard in her books by showing us how to redirect our innate power of imagination in a step-by-step manner in order to create the life we want.

The first time I used Shakti's *Creative Visualization Workbook*, I was waiting for my business partner to finish her meeting with a psychic. I sat outside in a park by the psychic's apartment, lost in my workbook for almost two hours. I wrote lists, created goals, and drew pictures about specific areas in which I wanted to create success. I was drawing a picture of the house I would buy my Mom, when my business partner called me into the office for my intuitive reading. I had been working on this page for almost 20 minutes, doodling little details about Mom's future property and really allowing my imagination to flow in a natural way. I closed my book and stored it in my backpack, zipped it up, and quickly went inside for my time slot. I had not sat with the psychic more than 60 seconds when she looked at me and said, "I don't know what you're worried about young man. You're going to buy your mother a house one day."

My mouth dropped open and my jaw hit the floor. Neither my partner nor the psychic saw or knew what I was doing outside while they were together.

In that exact moment, I realized the power of visualization and imagination. I felt great drawing and imagining with Shakti's books. I loved using the power of my Intuitive Intellect to create Mom's house in my thoughts, feelings, and imagination, then writing and drawing what I saw in my head onto the paper. I knew then and there with the psychic experience that my feelings and invisible imagination were an absolute reality moving from the nonphysical world into the physical world toward me.

Visualization and imagination are only BUT Blasters when we use them in hi-frequency formats. Feeling good, feeling great, or having Energetic Multiple Orgasmic Combustion Points are pure vibrations magnetizing more good and more greatness to us. All too often, people choose to imagine or visualize the worst-case scenario. In fact, entire libraries have been written on the dark side of life in every category imaginable. I am not suggesting these books and other materials have no merit; I am saying that we can really use more material empowering each other to share in the soul kiss of our pure desires and heartfelt aspirations, to shine a light on the positive aspects in life and to simply talk about what we do love and appreciate in our now perspectives.

Last year, while working on the cable television program *Perspectives,* created by Marissa Kelley, Marissa and I had long conversations about the essence of the show and its purpose. We filmed *Perspectives* for over a year, during which time I secretly pretended and imagined with focused feelings that we were filming a show for network television. Marissa, our host Ellen Dostal, David Tillman, and I went through wardrobe, makeup, hair, set list, and program lineups. With each step forward, I practiced visualization and imagination techniques. I appreciated everyone on the set—both in front of and behind the cameras—who worked hard to make the show a success.

Roughly six months into filming, representatives from the FOX Network contacted me about doing a show they were putting together. To make a long story short, I met with executive producers, creators, and the head of FOX Television in Los Angeles to discuss filming a test pilot. Weeks later, a film crew was assembled and together we filmed all types of shoots for nearly 12 hours.

My focused imagination about a house for Mom came back to me in a psychic's prediction mere moments after I wrote of it. The energy I was putting out to the Universe with the show *Perspectives* came back to me six months later in the form of the FOX Network calling. And what began as a small, two-page class outline about BIG BUTS has now manifested into this book.

George Bernard Shaw said, "Life isn't about finding yourself. Life is about creating yourself." Every day, I consciously choose to focus my imagination and visualization abilities into the areas of life that uplift, nurture, and serve me. I count blessings and look on the lighter side of life. I do this because it feels good to feel good. It feels good to have more solutions than problems and more positive things than negative things. It feels normal to focus on the light that I/we are than to focus my dominant attention into the dark. I believe we can uplift more people by standing and living in the light of our Soul Electricity.

Charles Lindbergh said, "It is the greatest shot of adrenaline to be doing what you've wanted to do so badly. You almost feel like you could fly without the plane." Appreciate your imagination and fly without the plane. Create positive realities in your imagination. Visualize a series of destinies that fit your wildest heaven-sent dreams. Write them, draw them, speak them, and share them with other people of like mind who support and appreciate your newfound desire to live the life you were born to enjoy.

BUT Blaster Twelve   Day Dreams and Night Dreams

> *"If you will practice being fictional for awhile, you will understand that fictional characters are sometimes more real than people with bodies and heartbeats."*
>
> —*Richard Bach*

Before writing this book, I was diligently working on a novel based on historical events in the mid 1800s. The book, *A Walk Between Worlds,* weaves a fiction and nonfiction tapestry together as one. For years, I heard authors say their fictional characters came to life in their dreams and daydreams, acting out their parts for the author to record. In other words, the writer had put such pure emotional focus on his or her characters that the fictional characters themselves took on lives of their own.

The first time I heard comments like these, I thought to myself, "That is ridiculous!" Later, I realized firsthand how true their comments were.

At the gym, on a treadmill, with my stereo headset blaring in my ears is one of my favorite avenues to connect and communicate with the fictional characters in *A Walk Between Worlds.* I pick music that fits the essence of the scene that comes to me in my daydreams and imagination. While on the treadmill, I hold on tightly to the machine, close my eyes, and allow the dream world to come to me easily. I often keep pad and pen with me in order to capture the story on paper before I forget the information.

One day, there were only three people in the gym: Gene Castellino, the owner; another client; and me. I was at another pivotal point in the story. On this day, I was listening to Patti La Belle's *Greatest Hits* CD as scenes from the novel drifted in and out of my light dream state. Suddenly, the scenes dramatically lifted off the pages of my imagination and melded into a more concrete version inside my mind's eye. I felt highly charged emotion pouring forth from my heart and solar plexus area. My body began to subtly vibrate internally. Right before my eyes, the image of a hundred characters chained together in a swamp astral projected back in order to capture an amazing overhead shot. In one moment, I was seeing and feeling my chapters unfold and in the next moment, I was seeing a famous director surrounded with dozens of high-powered lights, endless crew members, and hundreds of extras shooting the footage from my book and creating a movie. Looking closer, I even saw myself standing in the woods by the swamp with other crew members.

In the scene, my dream personality had a realization. My dream self knew the moment the sun began dropping behind the tree-lined everglades that the actors and extras in the swamp would be eaten up by mosquitoes. When the director yelled, "Cut!" in his megaphone, I expressed my concern about the mosquitoes to him. Acting quickly, he sent runners to get ointment before the mosquitoes descended on their buffet of actors and extras.

The next scene jumped to every one of us on the crew, including the director, quickly rubbing gobs of ointment on the actors and extras for two reasons. We didn't want them to get eaten alive, and the director wanted to get the early evening sunset shots.

Many of us were waist-deep in swamp water, rubbing the talent with ointment while preparing for the final couple of shots for the day. Some people complained about the ointment's smell and its greasy texture against their skin. We apologized, saying it was all we could find on short notice and reminded them it would keep the bugs off.

While quickly applying ointment to my last actor, someone reached around and grabbed my calf. Because I wasn't expecting it, I jumped, which caused me to open my eyes.

I was a little startled to be in Sherman Oaks in a gym and on a treadmill after experiencing such a vivid, imaginative journey. Instinctively, I turned my head to see who had touched my calf. Gene was standing beside my treadmill rubbing his two fingers together and smelling them with a look of confusion on his face. He turned to the client he was training and said, "No, it's not Eddie either."

Stunned, I asked Gene why he'd touched my leg. Gene replied that he and his client began to smell some type of an ointment fragrance. He said the strong smell came from out of nowhere, and they couldn't trace the source of it. After the two of them checked themselves for the strange scent, Gene decided to check me. He rubbed the back of my leg to see if I was the source of the ointment! After the fact, I realized the amazing power of our conscious dreams and imagination.

In 2002, I was in a gym in Southern California daydreaming with fictional characters I had created. The characters in my book, some fiction and some nonfiction, lived in the southeastern United States a century and a half earlier. Across a span of 150 years and some 2,000 miles, two men smelled the ointment my dream crew rubbed onto actors and extras in a movie that had not been made from a book I have yet to finish.

Any time we purely hold the essence of our dreams and imagination, the Universe knocks itself out to bring that feeling into physical manifestation. Nighttime dreams, in my opinion, are more powerful than our daydreams. Why? Because when we sleep we are in the land of pure energy. We have no distractions, and certainly no BIG BUTS. When our physical bodies are sleeping, our conscious thinking mind tiptoes to the back burner so our subconscious and super conscious can come out and play with our Heaven self.

We've all had premonitions and otherworldly experiences in our nighttime dreams. We can float, soar, fly, and create miracles in our dreams. We can future forecast and seek unlimited guidance directly from God Universe.

Nighttime dreams are BUT Free zones. In our dream experiences, our soul personality only enhances our strengths and our life purpose direction, sprinkling this knowledge into our daily lives like spiritually inspired fairy dust.

While writing her first book, *How To Be Happy,* Cynthia Richmond kept picturing the *Oprah* audience as the perfect customer for her book and what it offered. During this time, Cynthia had a dream in which she was watching *Oprah* on TV. During the show, Oprah held up Cynthia's book, looked into the camera, and said *How To Be Happy,* on the next *Oprah!*"

Some time later, Cynthia was actually on *Oprah* discussing a related topic. She gave Oprah her book during a commercial break. Oprah held Cynthia's book up and said, "How To Be Happy."

Even though the show Cynthia was on did not feature her new book, Cynthia can see and feel that her visualization + her imagination = a manifestation that reflected more of what is to come in her not-so-distant future. Cynthia's latest book, *Dream Power: Use Your Dreams to Change Your Life,* has given her national exposure as the country's leading dream expert. She has appeared on shows like *Oprah, The View, Politically Incorrect,* and *Leeza,* to name a few.

Cynthia is a beaming example of how we can use our daydreams and nighttime dreams as catalysts to create positive change in our daily lives. I have learned, sometimes the hard way, that if we do not consciously give our brain something to focus on, it will habitually repeat our old habits back to us over and over again.

If our old habits are low frequency, we will continue to create lo-frequency circumstances. It is important to put our best dream foot forward in order to create the life that we have dreamt of living. Heck, what do we have to lose? Being happy?

12

The BUT Blaster Workout

Over the years, enthusiastic people have emailed, phoned, and faxed a few of their favorite BUT Blasters. These are areas in their lives that lift them up from lo-frequency funks to hi-frequency results. Over time, their habits of worry, concern, fear, anxiety, and fret began to melt away as they made a conscious decision to pick thoughts and feelings that radiate in their **Solar Plexus Megaphone**®.

This is a list of contributions "straight from the horse's mouth" that will assist you in raising your mind and emotions from an average thought activity into the pure essence of your **Soul's Electricity**®.

I recommend you pick at least three points of focus each day. Do your first subject in the morning, the second in the middle of your day, and your last subject in the evening.

This list is designed to assist you in focusing on subjects that amplify good, positive emotions. Whenever possible, lock your Focused Feelings onto the subject that resonates with your desire to raise your vibration for 30 seconds to two minutes at a time. Hold the subject in your mind and in your Solar Plexus Megaphone®. Feel the animated essence of the subject you have chosen.

This "feel good" discipline can assist in eliminating your BIG BUT and over time can amplify and build you to more thought and feelings which, in turn, will promote and magnetize your dreams.

Let the BUT Blaster Games begin.

People Laughing	Natural Beauty	Expressing Humor
Newborn Babies	Smiles	Puppies or Kittens
Sincere People	Acts of Kindness	Happiness
Well-being	Joy	Win-Win Situations
Positive Outcomes	Pure Desire	A Soft Breeze
Crisp Morning Air	Radiant Dreaming	Music
Song	Dance	Favorite Quotes
Reading	Passion	Inspiration
Accomplishment	Standing Ovation	Meditation
Creativity	Appreciation	Déjà Vu
Clear Intention	Knowledge	Freedom
Sunlight	Moonlight	Starlight
Great Friendships	Cartoons	Sitcoms
Hilarious Jokes	Confidence	Self Love
Spirituality	Soul Focus	Feeling Supported
Divination	Allowing Good	Feeling Good
Abundance	Prosperity	Radiating God Self
Sincerity	Life Purpose	Ease
Synchronicity	Goose Bumps	Loving Memories
Intuition	Feeling Great	Decadent Food
Travel	Healing Journeys	Visualization
Reiki	Massage	Hot Showers

Rituals	Miracles	Counting Blessings
Chanting	Enlightenment	Afternoon Naps
Honesty	Feeling Special	Self Appreciation

Do you have a BUT Blaster suggestion to add to the list?

13

The Feel Good Life

Today, in this moment, make a conscious hi-frequency decision to move through your life knowing you are in the OVAL Mirror of life. This mirror is unconditional love, and it only says yes to your vibration 24/7. It supports your dreams, goals, and aspirations. It brings you solutions and clarity. And, at the exact same time, the OVAL Mirror supports your negative emotions, lo-frequency thoughts, and self-inflicted shortcomings, which, in turn, bring you more problems and obscurity.

Whatever "invisible" feelings you choose to radiate are reflected in the "invisible" OVAL Mirror, and the OVAL Mirror then manifests your feelings back to you physically. Do things, Think things, and Feel things inside that activate Good Feelings. This is a beautiful form of self-love that will enhance your life tenfold.

Create a prosperity commitment. Every moment you think of it, do a Feel Good Free-For-All ritual. Observe everything you can that makes you feel good. If there is not a pleasant physical environment around you that feels good, create the ideal environment in your imagination. Do this with the power of your Intuitive Intellect and beef it up with a ramped-up Energetic Multiple Orgasmic Combustion Point.

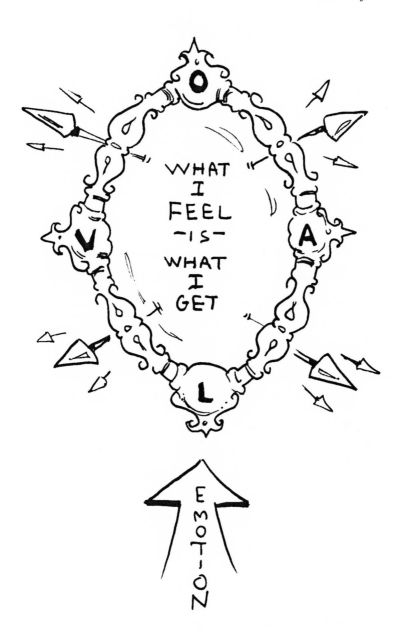

14

Your Soul Affirming Oath

It is hard to believe we have come to the end of our journey together. Though this is the completion of the mental material, I also feel it marks a new beginning. I think of this material as a pristine lake of crystal-clear consciousness; each new belief generated in your mind as a result of these pages is equivalent to dropping pebbles of pure intention into your new perspective, thus creating a new beginning using hi-frequency tools designed to enhance the quality of your life.

I thank you with all my heart and soul for taking this spiritual adventure with me. I am appreciative and grateful for our time together.

I want to close the book with an oath of intention. I soulfully suggest that you playfully recite this oath each morning as you awake before starting your day, and again each night before falling asleep. Remember the power and vibration of your Intuitive Intellect as you speak or think each word. Allow the feeling frequency of each word to resonate and vibrate purely inside of each and every atom, molecule and cell.

Why?

Because each night as we sleep, we merge into our soul consciousness and become the pure essence of the Universe, and each morning as we awaken, we are still strongly connected to our universal power. The longer we are physically awake, the more we choose to be distracted by mundane, insignificant things that do not serve our higher good.

Reciting this oath with the frequency your intuitive soul and your human intellect creates a masterful bridge of light over the pristine lake of consciousness. Think of each pebble of pure intention that you drop into the lake as aligning you with your much deserved life. As a result, you are leaving your BIG BUT behind and enhancing your love, money, and career.

Practice saying this light-hearted mantra for the next 30-to 45-day cycle or until you become consciously aware that you are observing pleasant things that make you feel good. Before you realize it, you will have developed a soulful habit of observing hi-frequency persons, places, and things in your physical world and in your mental thoughts and imagination.

Happy creating and blessings to you always! At last, your Soul Affirming Oath:

Today, I will consciously stand in the OVAL Mirror of life, applying the TAGS Technique in brilliant harmony with my Intuitive Intellect.

If I accidentally commit a Big BUT travesty, I will gladly employ the 1-2-3s of the B-U-T, Big BUT Stand-ins, or my AND Avalanches.

As a Soul Artist creating my life, I will feel good, laugh hard, and laugh often. I will get out in nature and listen to music that inspires and uplifts my Earth Self into my Heaven Self as ONE.

I will pray with a pure heart while using Vibratory Vocabulary that activates my Soul Electricity. I will dream, visualize, and imagine the best-case scenario while wearing my Thinking C.A.P.

I promise to give myself at least one to three Energetic Multiple Orgasmic Combustion Points a day until I graduate to one to three times an hour. I will start NOW! And so it is!

BUT Blaster References

Jeff Dannels has been in graphic design and marketing for over 15 years. He currently owns New Symmetry Design Studio in Los Angeles, providing print, logo, and web design services to a wide range of clients throughout North America. Find New Symmetry online at NewSymmetry.com.

Rev. Dr. Cynthia Cavalcanti is a writer and editor whose life mission entails helping other spiritual professionals in the process of articulating and publishing their message. She may be contacted in writing at: 30872 South Coast Highway, Box 302, Laguna Beach, CA 92651.

Robert Villegas knew he wanted to be an Artist at the age of eight. He studied art in college. In 1984 he had an opportunity to train as an amusement park caricature Artist at Knotts Berry Farm, Magic Mountain, The Queen Mary and is currently at Universal Studios Hollywood. Robert says, "I was blessed to have had an opportunity to work in animation as a background painter for a few years. One of Robert's shows was King of the Hill. Contact Robert at CoreShadow.com

Cynthia Richmond is a board certified behavioral therapist, columnist, author and speaker. She divides her time between writing her own books and articles and ghost writing and book doctoring for other writers. She specializes in dream work, helping others to improve their lives by understanding their dreams. Visit Cynthia's website at DreamPower.Net

Victor Benoun is the president of The Mortgage Source, Inc., a Southern California-based mortgage company. He has worked in real estate lending for twenty five years and has helped thousands of people in their dream to achieve home ownership. He may be reached at YourCastleNoHassle.com or VictorBenounCompany.com

Far as the Moon Productions, based in Los Angeles, creates unforgettable, award-winning movies and videos for clients nationwide. Partners Rose Wuyts-Wilson and Brian Wilson provide complete writing, photography and production services. Their motto is, "We make our clients happy, and our clients make us happy!" Reach them at FarAsTheMoonProductions.com

Abraham-Hicks Publications, ABRAHAM, a group of obviously evolved teachers, speak their broader Non-Physical perspective through the physical apparatus of Ester. Speaking to our level of comprehension, from their present moment to our now, through a series of loving, allowing, brilliant yet comprehensively simple, recordings in print and in sound—they guide us to a clear connection with our Inner Being. (The OVAL Mirror was inspired from the ABRAHAM teachings) For more information contact Abraham-Hicks.com

Chellie Campbell has combined her gift for public speaking with her financial expertise to create the Financial Stress Reduction® Workshop. This eight-week series, designed to help people make more money and have more time off for fun, quickly became a rousing success. Speaking from the heart of her own personal obstacles to creating abundance, and how she used the tools in her book *The Wealthy Spirit* to overcome them, she has helped thousands of people achieve a wealthy spirit and healthy balance in their lives. She can be reached at Chellie.com

John Livesay has been selling for over 20 years in the advertising and computer industries. He is the West Coast Director for *W* magazine. His advertising clients include Nike, Gap, Banana Republic, Jaguar, Lexus and Infiniti. As a member of the National Speakers Association, he is a motivational speaker who demonstrates how anyone can incorporate integrity, passion and joy into their professional and personal lives for optimal success. He lives in Los Angeles. He may be contacted at JohnLivesay.com

Karen Drucker is one of the preeminent visionary vocalists in the New Thought world today. Combining her multiple talents as singer, songwriter, comedienne and motivational speaker, Karen creates an opportunity for audiences everywhere to laugh, reflect and remember the truth of who they are. Performing songs from many of her best-selling recordings, you'll soon come to know why so many notables from motivational psychologist Joan Borysenko to best-selling author SARK call her simply "the best." Contact her at KarenDrucker.com

The Caster features complete state-by-state listings of Casting Directors addresses and phone numbers, (and their astrological signs) current show breakdowns of who's casting what, survival information about SAG, AFTRA, Equity, the DGA, the WGA, and more! While the

Power Agent features constantly updated directory of Agents addresses and phone numbers (talent, literary, modeling, and more) with their astrological signs. Hollywood Insiders give their Secrets of Success to Actors, Directors, Models, Producers, and Writers. Contact the Caster and Power Agent Magazines at InsideHollywoodsHead.com

David Ault has been in the forefront of visionary music for the past 20 years. Considered one of the true pioneers in New Thought music, this Renaissance man has gone on to become a highly acclaimed minister, lecturer and now, best-selling author. With focus on the art of appreciation, honoring the call of Spirit and reconnecting to our feelings, this master storyteller and motivator will create a space for transformations and healing you'll never forget. Contact: DavidAult.com

Adam Abraham is the Author of *I AM My Body, NOT!* and publisher. Adam welcomes you to Phaelos Books & Mediawerks where humanism, intelligence, cooperation, transformation, positivism, self-reliance, hope, energy, and love are guiding principles of our nondenominational phaelosophy. Through publishing, media (music, video), and merchandising, let's celebrate the best of life together. For more information contact Phaelos.com

Lauren Soloman guides her clients along the journey of creating a personal image that is uniquely their own. She is frequently featured in print, television and radio as a subject matter expert and image industry spokesperson. Lauren is the author of *Image Matters!* And you can find Lauren at LSimage.com.

Mary Jo Matsumoto designs have appeared on Oprah, Entertainment Tonight, and the 2004 Oscars. Currently she is working on a book entitled *The Feminine Evolution,* which encourages a celebration of femininity as the next step for women everywhere. The Mary Jo Matsumoto couture clothing line launches in October 2004. For more information contact: Mary Jo Matsumoto (310) 203-8803 or MaryJoMatsumoto.com

Mary Ann Halpin dances while she shoots. "I love to photograph the spirit of people and bring the best out of them, their fun, their liveliness. That makes me dance." Although known for her celebrity portraits, albums and CD covers, Halpin has received acclaim for revealing everything from the glamorous beauty of Hollywood and the exquisite glow of pregnancy to the heartbreaking despair of Skid Row. She is the author of *Pregnant Goddesshood: A Celebration of Life*. For more information contact: MaryAnnHalpin.com

Jacquie Jordon, Inc. came together in an effort to create a visionary company that seeks to educate, enlighten and entertain the masses with the highest level of integrity. Our "boutique" production company, media consulting and coaching firm promises to challenge us spiritually, engage us creatively, and to honor ourselves as well as others in order to bring about fulfillment and unlimited abundance. For more information contact JacquieJordan.com.

Electric Kites, LLC—Life Coaching for Companies and Individuals. Electric Kites is passionate, adventurous and unexpected. They take risks. In their private coaching, as well as their public workshops, Electric Kites demonstrates a decided talent for delivering extraordinary change while honoring a willingness to play. Through goal setting, accountability, and coaching towards perspective shifts, Electric Kites believes in securing all individuals with a strong sense of themselves and their personal vision so that they glide into a new experience of freedom and power. Electric Kites is a conduit connecting you with that wonderful feeling of peace along with the exhilaration of progress. Contact Melissa McFarlane, CPCC at ElectricKites.com

About the Author

Eddie Conner is a native of North Carolina. Intuitive since childhood, he was immediately fascinated with metaphysics and the energetic dynamics that create and govern our lives. Studying these behavior patterns activated and enhanced his innate psychic abilities.

An avid student of spirituality and the New Age movement, Eddie soon became an Usui Reiki practitioner, a Master Teacher in Magnified Healing, and a Teri-Mai™ Reiki Master. Eddie's imagination and conscious dreaming techniques became a physical reality when the entertainment community came-a-calling in 1995. Since then, Eddie has enjoyed the amazing opportunity to work personally and professionally with many of Hollywood's elite.

Eddie is a contributing author to the bestsellers *More Hot Chocolate for the Mystical Soul* and *Hot Chocolate for the Mystical Teenage Soul*, as well as a contributing writer for *The Power Agent, The Caster,* and *MetaArts.com* magazines.

He is a popular speaker, humorist, seminar leader, and Soul Intuitive. He facilitates spiritual travel adventures and world tours to South America, the Far East, and the Mexican Riviera. Eddie and his teeny weenie *BUT* live in Los Angeles. For more information, see www.EddieConner.com.

0-595-32181-X

Printed in the United States
86483LV00004B/248/A

9 780595 321810